The Waiting Country

Mike Nicol was born in 1951, and has worked as a journalist since 1974. His previous books include the novels *The Powers That Be*, *This Day and Age* and *Horseman*, and a non-fiction account of black journalists in the 1950s, *A Good-Looking Corpse*. He has also published two volumes of poetry. He lives at Muizenberg on the Cape peninsula.

'A writer whose understanding of and compassion for humankind is evident in every paragraph . . . a word wizard, a master storyteller.' – *Cape Times*

By the same author

Fiction
The Powers That Be
This Day and Age
Horseman

Non-Fiction
A Good-Looking Corpse

The Waiting Country

A South African Witness

MIKE NICOL

VICTOR GOLLANCZ

LONDON

First published in Great Britain 1995
by Victor Gollancz
A Division of the Cassell group
Wellington House, 125 Strand, London WC2R 0BB

A Gollancz Paperback original

A catalogue record for this book is
available from the British Library.

ISBN 0 575 05915 X

Typeset in Great Britain at
The Spartan Press Ltd, Lymington, Hants
Printed in Finland by Werner Söderström Oy

Contents

Abbreviations

ANC	African National Congress
APLA	Azanian People's Liberation Army
AWB	Afrikaner Weerstandsbeweging
BBC	British Broadcasting Corporation
COSATU	Congress of South African Trade Unions
DTP	Desktop publishing
IEC	Independent Electoral Commission
MK	Umkhonto we Sizwe
NP	National Party
PAC	Pan Africanist Congress
PLO	Palestine Liberation Organization
PWV	Pretoria Witwatersrand Vereeniging complex (now Gauteng)
SABC	South African Broadcasting Corporation
UMR	Umvoti Mounted Rifles
UNISA	University of South Africa
USA	United States of America
WAM	World Apartheid Movement

Acknowledgements

For their comments and ideas I would like to thank Robert Brookes, Peter and Barbara Fairhead, Piet Human and Dene Smuts; and particularly I am grateful to Linda Human for her insights and comments on the manuscript. And for their help in finding obscure documents, I owe thanks to the librarians at the Cory Library, Grahamstown, the South African Library, Cape Town, and the South African Archives, Pietermaritzburg. I am indebted to Quentin Cornelius, Michael January and Ginn Fourie for retelling their accounts of the Heidelberg Tavern attack, and to Emma and Howard for their frankness. Also my thanks to Vicki Harris at Gollancz for presenting an opportunity to write this. Finally, and as always, I owe much to Jill Gallimore for her love and support, and for the arcane references she found and the books she suggested I read.

1

It is June 1994. I sit here in my red room with its books and stare at the two photographs caught in wide black frames upon the wall and think of how to begin this story. I look first at the photograph by David Goldblatt which is of a graveyard in a vast plain. A low wall made from pre-cast slabs of decorated concrete fronts the cemetery. It speaks of crassness and a poverty of imagination. Behind this a wire fence forms the rest of the rectangle dividing the small ground of the dead from the large empty ground of the living. Over the gate is a standard that reads: ONS VIR JOU SUID AFRIKA. It is a phrase out of what used to be the only official national anthem. It means that we will sacrifice our lives for our motherland, South Africa. The 'we' means young white soldiers. Since 10 May we have started singing two national anthems. We sing them at soccer matches and rugby matches and other occasions of national importance. This other national anthem is 'Nkosi Sikelel' iAfrika', 'God Bless Africa'. It has been the na-tional anthem for most people in this country for years and years.

The second photograph, taken in the mid-Eighties, is by Eric Miller and shows Cosatu House at night being raided by the police. Miller had positioned himself in a building opposite the trade union's headquarters and graphically composed a picture of four well-lit floors. The unionists have been made to stand against the windows with their arms up as if they are worshipping. They are back-lit and the effect is dramatic. Policemen with automatic weapons can be seen behind them. In some other rooms police are searching through files.

I sit in this red room and stare at the photographs and remember incidents and stories that I need to tell. Stories from distant places that were told by the people and by the stones and by the emptiness that was not always emptiness. Stories I have taken in and made part of what it is to live here. Stories I use to explain and interpret what is happening or what I think is happening. And sometimes they do this and sometimes they resound inexplicably, angrily, offering nothing but themselves. And sometimes, where once I understood, later I am faced with incomprehension. But still I need to tell, to order, to arrange these fragments into a form that may show how we live now. I think of them as footnotes to a history of these days. These days when history is so much with us; when sometimes I am truly afraid and when sometimes I know what is happening is unique.

I suppose that in the end all we really have are the stories. A ship sails into Table Bay and centuries of conflict begin. A man defends his own and his people are decimated. The prisoner becomes the president. And other stories that are kept hidden and secret and are passed on like confessions: We hanged three men who were walking down the road. With automatic fire we killed three young women drinking in a pub. These stories have to be told and retold because in the telling and the remembering and the not forgetting we may be able to create a narrative of our lives.

This, then, is a story about an election and an inauguration and the days of celebration, and some of the events around this time, and some events that belong to history but whose presence is still palpable.

It is a narrative without a beginning or a middle or an end. The beginning could have been any detail other than the one it is, and the end is not an end. The story is open. I cannot say: 'And they lived happily ever after.'

It is June 1994. I live in Muizenberg on the Cape peninsula at what is not, but feels like it is, the very end of Africa. It is winter. The barometer reads 1,000 millibars. Yesterday a hot wind blew from the mountains, drying out the moisture in our eyes. Today it rains.

The peninsula has a dangerous beauty. It is pristine on a fine day; dramatic in a storm. Sometimes it does not seem to be a part of Africa. It becomes a fantasy land, an island somewhere to the side of the continent. It is an illusion which is enhanced by the vineyards, the soft green pastures, the gabled farmhouses, the corners of colonial architecture in the older parts of the city.

Yet it is still Africa, and it bears witness to the hardships of Africa. Just forty kilometres away is the township of Khayelitsha with its shacklands and its poverty and its violence. A violence that at times has been little short of civil war. Things are not quite so bad now. But before the election we lived in split realities: hearing eye-witness reports of riots and police shootings, and political assassinations, and acts of outright banditry, while our own streets were peaceful and the mountains towered pink and misty behind these chilling conversations. This was our context; and, no matter how ordinary and funny and warming and seductive each day was, we had to remember it – always.

I can say things are not as bad now but I must also say that this is June 1994. In the coming months that statement may no longer be valid. On the other hand, who would have said that the elections would be peaceful and that the violence would drop off? Maybe things will get better. I do not know.

This place where I live, Muizenberg, is a collection of run-down houses and shops on the coast of False Bay about thirty kilometres south of Cape Town. Yet it is idyllic. The beach is three minutes' walk away. At low tide it offers a sweep of white sand extending unbroken for five kilometres to the east. To the west is the mountain. A few hundred metres to the north is a large vlei – a tract of swampland and open water where sometimes on still winter afternoons we drift about in a canoe. Overhead wheel giant pelicans, kingfishers drop into the water after minnows, carp break the surface chasing long-legged flies.

Muizenberg is swept by a summer wind, the 'south-easter', which is as disturbing as the mistral or *meltemi*. There have been times when it has blown solidly for ten or twelve days and brought the edge of violence up beneath the surface of the skin. Great swathes of salt roar across the mountain, the windowpanes blur, there is a constant noise and we wander listlessly about the house wondering when it is going to end.

I live here because once the houses were cheap and because each spring the whales come to the bay. I live here because the streets are narrow and the houses are terraces or semis that owe their architecture to Lithuania and Victorian England and the whaling villages of Norway. But this is not a quaint village. It was and still is partly a neighbourhood of poor whites and poor coloureds and poor blacks who sit on the stoeps drinking cheap wine from mugs. The men wear vests and shorts; the women are

14

in curlers and petticoats. They exist from one disability pension payout to the next, from one bottle of brandy to the next. But it is also a neighbourhood of artists and writers and cartoonists and dance teachers and potters and sculptors and jazz musicians. In its narrow back streets are four of Cape Town's better restaurants. It has late-night pubs and erratic jazz dens where the big names can be heard for the price of a beer. It is the way both these sides coexist that attracts me.

When we moved here the house stank of sixty years of boiled cabbage and dead rats decaying beneath the floorboards. Next door lived three violent and drunken people who would swear and shout and assault one another for half an hour each evening before collapsing. We would grit our teeth and wait for the quiet which heralded their oblivion. They went. Others came. It is now the home of Harry, a metal-sculptor.

Five years ago a coloured family moved into a house up the street. They could have been arrested for contravening the Group Areas Act, which restricted people to racially designated regions, but nobody has ever bothered much about that in Muizenberg. It was the first time the family had lived in what was classified a white area.

'You know,' they said, 'we just don't understand the way you whites live. It's all very nice here but this is the first time we've ever had to put up with a shebeen next door, a brothel over the road, and a drug den behind us.'

That there are a brothel, a shebeen and a drug den is one of the facts about life in the poorer parts of the city. The drug den is gone now although the brothel and shebeen still trade.

Yet Muizenberg is not a violent place. There may be former convicts in the boarding houses, and the population of itinerants, alcoholics and street children is high, but it is safe to walk in the streets at all hours of the night. These days we have a security grille on the back door and burglar bars at some of the windows, but in the country's other major cities people live with guard dogs and high fences strung with coils of barbed wire and sleep with magnum pistols beneath their pillows. They pay armed-response units to patrol the streets. In Muizenberg we live without this paranoia.

However, there is always something to give the lie. In our twelve years here two shopkeepers have been murdered. The one was an elderly barber. About seven years ago he was stabbed to death for the R20 change he had in his till. The other was Mr Adams. In November last year he was shot for the day's takings of about R600, or £110.

Mr Adams ran a corner café, a corner shop that was open seven days a week from early morning until late at night and sold soft drinks, bread, polony, groceries, frozen vegetables, newspapers, cigarettes, magazines, nail varnish, toys, fishing bait and beach umbrellas. Mons Tuck Shop, it was called. It was dim, lit by flickering fluorescent lights. Down one wall were glass cases of cheap watches and junk jewellery. There were racks of old magazines. The linoleum on the floor had been trodden through to the concrete. Beside the door stood three video-game machines endlessly flashing and pinging even when there were no children operating them. There was a smell of rancid polony in the shop.

About five years ago Mr Adams received in the mail a medal from the then Soviet President, Mikhail Gorbachev, in recognition of his efforts in helping Russian soldiers during the Second World War. He used to show it to me every time I bought a newspaper.

Mrs Adams had other obsessions. One Saturday morning

in her shop she grabbed me by the arm and said, 'The birds aren't singing. Do you know what it means when the birds aren't singing?'

I shook my head.

'It's an asteroid shower,' she whispered. 'That's why they're not singing.'

I looked at her, expecting further explanations, but I did not get any. She took my money and hummed tunelessly. When I didn't move away she said, 'That's all right, dear, there's no change.'

He is dead now. And she has gone to live with her children. These days a second-hand furniture dealer trades from that shop.

I give these details to establish where this is and when.

The story I thought about most frequently during the run-up to the election, during those brittle March and April days, concerns a man called Francisco d'Almeida, who was the first Portuguese viceroy in India. I thought that what he did was arrogant and stupid and showed no wisdom. I thought that men like Mangope of Bophuthatswana and Buthelezi of kwaZulu were behaving in the same way. I felt sad when I first read the story of d'Almeida. I felt that we, the people of this subcontinent, might never do anything right.

As the story goes, sometime in 1510, after a career of colonial conquest in Asia and along the East African coast, d'Almeida was sailing home to Portugal, no doubt anticipating honours and accolades and the final quiet years of his life. He put in at what is now Table Bay to revictual for the long haul to Lisbon. His men went ashore to trade with the Khoikhoi. What happened is unclear but they got into a dispute with the Khoi and felt so aggrieved by this that they persuaded the viceroy to mount a punitive expedition.

17

Perhaps a wiser man would have sailed away, dismissing the incident as a misunderstanding. But d'Almeida believed some injustice had to be redressed. His war party, armed with swords and lances, was rowed to the beach.

They marched to the Khoi settlement and, according to the record, tried to snatch the children as hostages. This naturally enraged the Khoi, who retaliated with such fury that the war party was routed. The Portuguese fled to the beach, only to discover that their boats had returned to sea to escape the relentless breakers. Here, in the shallows, they were slaughtered by men who, one survivor said, 'move so lightly they seem as birds'. By the time the boats came back in, fifty Portuguese, including d'Almeida, lay dead. Almost all the rest were severely wounded.

Some 140 years later the Dutch arrived to establish a refreshment station. So began the history of the colonization of southern Africa. In the process the Khoikhoi nation would be wiped out by wars, slavery and disease.

It is this history which has created the restive souls I call the Maleficents, who, metaphorically, can be seen at work in our society today.

I do not know when I first imagined the Maleficents because I cannot remember when I first read these paragraphs in Eve Palmer's book *The Plains of Camdeboo*. But I know that they have been with me ever since:

The colonists soon learned to regard the Bushmen as vermin, the most dangerous animals of all. In the 1790s a Graaff-Reinet farmer, when asked if he had found the Bushmen troublesome on the road, replied 'with as much composure and indifference as if he had been speaking of partridges' that he had only shot four. [The explorer

18

John] Barrow claimed that one colonist had boasted to him that he himself had killed nearly three hundred.

It was not only the Dutch colonists who regarded the Bushman as game. Le Vaillant, the French ornithologist, for example, hunted Bushmen . . . He had pitched his camp in excruciating heat in an open spot so that the Bushmen should not surprise him, and his Hottentots [Khoikhoi] kept constant watch, for, he said, 'A Hottentot dreads a Boschman much more than a lion.' From here he hunted them, and although he admired the way they flew over the rocks with the nimbleness of monkeys, it did not stop him from shooting at them.

An English farmer recorded that as a child he had seen his father and two Boers go out to shoot a Bushman. It is a gallant and pitiful story that must have been repeated many times in the Karoo. The Bushman had dug a hole for himself and in this, part of the veld as always, he lay shooting his arrows at the three men. They advanced slowly towards him, protected by an enormous shield of double ox-hide. The farmer in the middle held this, and the two on either side their rifles, which they fired as they walked, and as they moved they knew that one touch of a [poisoned] arrow in an unguarded foot or hand, and they were dead men. An arrow did indeed pierce one man's hat, but he was uninjured. The Bushman was finally killed, and when they examined his little body they found he had cut through the skin of his finger-tips with the constant pulling of his bow-string.

Farmers hunted the Bushmen in small groups, or in commandos. Barrow says that one such party near Graaff-Reinet 'prepared themselves for the enterprise by singing three or four hymns by William Sluiter and drinking each a glass of brandy.' They probably needed both.

Maybe I was twenty or twenty-one when I first read this. I remember afterwards trying to write a poem about aggrieved souls wandering in the limbo of a barren landscape waiting to exact their revenge. The landscape I imagined them in was the Karoo.

The Karoo is the heart of the country and the landscape within us. Once, in the late afternoon, I drove into its night with *The War of the Worlds* playing loudly.

'No, Nathaniel, no, there must be more to life,' sang Julie Covington.

I passed over plains of black scrub and black rocks where granite outcrops rose alone and randomly in witness to the eons of conflagration. The plains had no end: night came on them from the east and in the west a thin red line was ruled between the clouds and the earth. Sometimes a flame seared through the sky and sometimes it burned upon the ground.

The road was empty: this was the beginning and the end of the world. On the tape, Julie Covington sang that there had to be a way we could restore to our lives the light that we had lost.

There was rain about. Dark, isolated downpours that stood like solid pillars on the veld. They stood there and then disappeared. They were tangible in this moment and invisible in the next. Or they moved across the vastness, floating on long tendrils, seeming not to give succour but to suck from the ground its life. Out of them struck lightning. Within them rolled thunder.

I switched off the music. I was no longer certain that I drove on a road that would lead to towns.

Such is the world of the Maleficents. I call them this because they belong in a graphic novel concerned with vengeance and the last days. In such novels South Africa is often a place of destruction after a terrible race war. It is a stereotypical way of depicting this country. In the graphic novel *New Statesmen*, for instance, are illustrations of wasted landscapes and anguished heads and skulls super-imposed on the map of Africa. The caption reads: 'The

Afrikaaner Front murdered three ANC leaders at a rally in Johannesburg, and [the] president panicked and brought in the troops. It turned into a race war.' This is the future others have read into our story.

The Maleficents' ranks are made up of those who have been viciously slaughtered here, this century, last century, the centuries before. I imagine how at death they must gather in the bitter reaches of the karoo among the baked rocks and in the wind that rises white from the land. They wander here, in groups or alone, some with spears and bows and arrows, some with muskets, some with modern weapons. They are worn thin from the bitter cold of winter and the summer's searing heat; their bones show through; their faces have flaked into skulls.

On a rock wall in the Drakensberg Mountains they left the first message of why they would return. They showed how men on horses firing flintlock rifles came among them and slaughtered them. There was no escape from the rifles. The bullets are shown reaching out in long lines to strike the fleeing people. It is a scene of chaos: cattle mill about, and the people run and fall and stagger as the bullets burst into them. The horsemen come on relentlessly, remorselessly. There is no pause in what they are doing. They are going to annihilate. They are going to exterminate.

But this is not only a depiction of a violence. In it is a shaman in a deep trance bleeding from the nose and with two long emanations protruding from his head as his spirit leaves his body. He is beginning to use his supernatural powers to control and combat the intruders. In a way, he is warning of the return.

There are three Maleficents in the National Gallery in Cape Town. The way I see it, the sculptor Jane Alexander must have gone into the karoo and come back with them. They are life-size figures. They wait in the gallery seated on a bench. Their faces are distorted as the skin has started to melt and decay. Their mouths have disappeared. But their eyes have enlarged: gone huge, brown, glassy from looking always into the distance. In places their spines have broken through the flesh; you can see the plates of their skulls. They have grown horns.

They returned here in the harsh days of 1986. It was that year Winnie Mandela said, 'Together, hand in hand, with our boxes of matches and our necklaces we shall liberate this land.' We were under a state of emergency then. 'The Butcher Boys' (which is the title of Alexander's sculpture) were everywhere abroad. Vengeance had driven them mad. They were blood-crazed and could not stop what they were doing. Everyone was a victim. There was no sanction to what they did: no morality, or justice, or divine retribution; there was just gratuitous killing.

'The Butcher Boys' were part of Alexander's thesis for her Master of Arts degree and also appeared in some photo collages she made. I have one photograph of the three sitting in a narrow tiled corridor illuminated by stark fluorescent light. They sit as they always sit: the one with his legs crossed, bending forward, his arms resting on his knee. He looks up. He seems relaxed. Quite content to wait. The middle figure is tense: he stares fixedly at the wall, the muscles across his chest are tight, the veins in his arms raised, his hands rigid along his thighs. The third, the one with raised horns, sits almost defensively: his legs are parallel, his knees together, but his left shoulder is pulled forward like a shield. His hands grip the edge of the bench. Behind them on a door is a message: BY THE END OF TODAY YOU ARE GOING TO NEED US.

As with the Bushman depiction this collage is more complex than it seems: the tiled corridor comes from the London Underground, and the message was once the slogan of a British insurance company. Knowing this makes it worse somehow: the ramifications multiply and there is no simplicity left, no right and wrong.

Which is why I think the Maleficents have gone beyond vengeance. They have shadowed our lives constantly in the last years, demanding more and more blood. It is now mayhem they want.

In the weeks leading up to the election I was often fearful. There seemed to be so much killing. Massacres. Violent crimes. Murders. I would sit quietly in the pink depths of my house, aware of noises lifting off the street, or the children playing next door, or the neighbour's too loud television hysterical with news, and I would see them coming.

And yet, and yet . . .

Despite the litany of dead, right up to a bomb that killed nine people in Johannesburg on the Sunday before election week, I did not fear outright civil war. I still believed it would be all right. Despite the hundreds of foreign journalists and television crews waiting for the carnage to start, I still felt it would not. They might be vultures circling down before a lion's kill . . . They might come to rest in the trees: huge, hooded, their eyes unblinking. But there was not going to be a kill.

On election day we switched on the radio at seven in the morning. We needed to know what was happening: that there had not been another bomb or what has become known as a 'drive-by' – the sort of minibus-taxi killing that fills me with horror. What we heard was how people had walked for miles through the dark and bush to get to the polling stations and how they stood there in a fierce autumn sun sometimes for seven hours without food, without water, without toilets as they waited to draw their crosses. We were told of people who broke into tears afterwards, how they sobbed in one another's arms at the simplicity of what they had done. We heard of a man who had come to vote for Jan Smuts and who left in disgust when told his party was not standing, had been defunct for seventeen years and Smuts himself dead since 1950. We needed to hear all these stories. We sat and listened to the young man who had carried his grandmother to vote, of five-kilometre-long queues, of convoys of buses and taxis loaded with mostly silent, earnest voters. We let our tears well up in sympathy with those who could not stop the emotion, who had thought they would never do this in their lives.

At midday I went down to the pavilion on the beach-front that was my local voting station. The queue snaked back and forth across the parking lot. Some said they had been standing there for well over two hours. Here in the Cape people were cold and wet from the squalls blowing out of the north-west. And, given the size of the crowd, the atmosphere was subdued, solemn even. Double-decker buses were bringing people from Khayelitsha, where a number of polling points had not opened, and the queue lengthened by hundreds in a matter of minutes. I joined a group of bystanders. Among them was Philip, who works as a petrol-pump attendant at a nearby filling station.

'Have you voted?' I asked.

'Early, early. At seven o'clock. And you?'

I shook my head.

'Hey,' he laughed. 'It's going to take you hours.'

We swapped news on the voting. A group of ANC supporters draped in their party's colours came swaggering past. They were drinking from a quart bottle of beer, passing it playfully among themselves. 'Free choice. Free choice,' they called out at us. And went on, in their cheerfulness completely at odds with the voters who stood like pilgrims come to pay homage at a shrine.

And then Philip said, 'This is good. This is very good.'

Which are words often used to describe pleasure but they meant a lot more now. They meant 'good' in a moral sense and in a historical sense and in a sense that language cannot define. What he meant, I think, was a feeling that cannot be articulated and probably should never be articulated if it is to remain somehow uncontaminated. It contained in it a moment that was like a stone but also was tender: a moment that was good.

It was part of a phrase so many used when they voted that day: It felt so good, they said. And they would repeat it, clutching the words to themselves the way children hold toys.

Perhaps they felt that something had happened that was contrary to all their expectations, maybe even contrary to what they had come to think of as history. This 'something' was the equality implicit in the act of voting.

Philip grinned at me: 'Go and join the queue.'

'Later,' I said, 'later,' and raised a hand in a gesture of parting, and went towards the beach, exhilarated but also daunted by the thought of those lives that had been denied such a day as this.

I walked down to the water's edge where some seagulls were worrying at the carcass of a dead seal that had washed up on the tide. The sea was flat, grey, scudded with foam peeling back from the small breakers. Around the bay the mountains were dark and the clouds down on them. In the distance a lone figure came along the beach but otherwise it was deserted. And behind the pavilion wall history was enacting one of its rare quiet moments.

*

25

Later in the afternoon we drove with two friends to the most southerly voting station on the peninsula, at the Camel Rock Café. All the way the cloud was low and now a fog came off the Atlantic: somehow it seemed appropriate, this sense of going to some small place at the end of the mist. In the car we were exuberant: laughing, joking, recounting anecdotes from the day, wanting to make this an occasion to remember. Wanting to make it more than just another day in the country's history, as it would become. We wanted to make it ours as well. After all, it was the first time in her life that Jill would be voting. She was apprehensive, aware of the moment, anxious that she might do something wrong. And I had resolved that this time I would not spoil my vote as I had done in previous elections.

The Camel Rock Café, rather obviously, takes its name from the shape of a clump of rocks beside the road. As a child in the Fifties I can remember going there for tea and cream scones. In those days the National Party had not yet been in power for a decade but already they had enacted the most serious of the apartheid legislation: the Prohibition of Mixed Marriages Act, the Population Registration Act, Group Areas Act, Bantu Authorities Act, Bantu Education Act, Natives Resettlement Act . . . The list was long and thorough. In response there had been boycotts, protests, defiance campaigns, riots, deaths, detentions, bannings. Prime Minister Malan was in office. Nelson Mandela was a young lawyer in Johannesburg.

As we drove up the thought occurred that I had been to the Camel Rock Café for tea and cream scones at least once during the regimes of Verwoerd, Vorster, Botha and de Klerk. Which may seem a flippant thought, but it contains in it, too, a horrible truth: the acknowledgement of how some lives go on so trivially when others are faced with pain and suffering. As those men wielded the Suppression of Communism Act, or the Terrorism Act, or declared states of emergency, or played out the final years of white rule, the Camel Rock Café had been here serving its cream teas. In that time the ANC had been banned and unbanned. Nelson Mandela had been found guilty of treason, had served twenty-seven years of a life sentence, most of it on the notorious Robben Island. Had been released and was soon to be president. In one sense what the Camel Rock Café represented was ordinary and constant and it was a part of life that had been and was not going to change. Even as I changed from child to teenager to young man, to the forty-two-year-old come now to vote, the Camel Rock Café had stayed the same. It was one of those small consistencies not often to be found in South Africa.

There was no queue here. As we came up the steps two police officers glanced wanly at us. If they were carrying weapons they were well hidden beneath their trench coats. At the door a young man with the collars of his tweed jacket pulled up against the wind ushered us in one at a time. Jill was first and Peter was teasing her gently. Barbara and I stood quietly behind them. Waiting, I looked out over a sea in turmoil and at the sky rolling in huge and dark. I enjoyed the bleakness; its beauty seemed so dangerous, so mesmerizing.

Then the monitor waved me inside. Above the election officials was a dinner menu written on a blackboard advertising leek and potato soup, grilled yellowtail, apple crumble, coffee. But apart from that the interior did not look like a café. It looked more like a grim room for processing refugees fleeing some devastating civil war. The lights were dim. The place stank of cigarette smoke. Four men in overcoats talked at a table in the corner. Their ashtray was full; their coffee mugs were stained with runs of brown liquid. Before me at their desks sat six officials. They were unsmiling, their faces numbed by the long day. The first one watched me enter, her expression blank, her response now automatic. She asked for my identity book and I gave it. She looked at the photograph and then up at my face and there was in her eyes that bored response perfected by guards at border posts. She pushed the document towards me, confirming that I still had something of the long-haired, smooth-featured, twenty-five-year-old in my face. The infra-red checking, the dabbing of my fingers with invisible ink took their course. I was handed a voting form and went into a booth. I picked up the pencil that was well chewed and attached to the makeshift desk by a length of string and searched through the list of seventeen parties. Next to each was a smiling face: some well known, most strangers who would soon disappear again. I put my cross, quickly, trying not to agonize about it yet again. Weeks ago I had made a decision and now kept to it. I looked up at the menu while I refolded the paper. At some time soon, I realized, when Mandela was in the high office, I would have to come back to the Camel Rock Café and order tea and cream scones with apricot jam.

As we left, Jill needed to speak, needed to say: 'I'm a voter. It's the first time I've voted.' The young man in the thin jacket gave her a wide smile. 'Me too,' he said. 'It was my first time too.' The difference was that Jill could have done it before if she had wanted to. But he could not have. Right now the difference did not matter.

That evening we had a phone call from our friend Brenda, who runs a restaurant at the bottom of a long rutted road on the Natal south coast. It is a part of the country that has been blooded by the ANC/Inkatha war and is also a stronghold for AWB thugs. But Brenda has more trouble with the black mamba snakes than she does with the poisonous end of politics. Like Jill she emigrated here from England in the late Sixties; like Jill she had never voted before.

'It was fantastic,' she said. 'It was amazing. It just felt so good. And on the way back home I drove past a woman walking and you know I never stop, well I stopped. I thought, No, not today. So I turned round and went back and picked her up and drove her home.'

Later we had another telephone call. This time from Lynette, a friend in England who sounded concerned that what she had heard on the news might not reflect the true story. She had recently spent a three-week holiday here. On the day she arrived the local newspaper carried a large picture on the front page of three men in khaki shirts and shorts lying dead beside their Mercedes Benz. They were members of an AWB commando executed during the Bophuthatswana revolution.

'Is everything all right?' she asked now.

I told her about Philip. I told her about dignity, about equality. But the words sounded inadequate, filled with too much sentimentality, although I could hear her sympathetic reaction. But still, I thought, how do I tell this to someone who has been able to vote from the moment she turned eighteen, and who never questioned this right, who expected it? There was only one way: to describe the queues and the hours people waited. In this was the meaning of being enfranchised.

2

I have no clear remembrance of the days that followed. There is a blur about them. They started out with such expectations and ended in such farce. I remember that the radios were on constantly: one in the kitchen, one in the sitting room, and that the voices of anchorwomen Shado Twala and Patricia Glyn followed us about the house. We were conscious of passing the time. We read half-heartedly, always alert for some stray piece of news. We drank endless cups of coffee. Through binoculars we watched walkers on the bright mountain. We watched climbers, like four-legged arachnids, slide about the granite faces. And we felt, like them, that we were fighting a pressure that would tear us away into oblivion if we missed the slightest news. And yet I cannot remember much more than these insignificant details. They were days out of time. Radio and television turned the whole country into a small community. For Saturday, Sunday, Monday, Tuesday we were a community bound by the voices of Shado and Patricia. Which was how we waited for the election results. Listening to Shado and Patricia. They never seemed to sleep. They were always there, spinning out the empty hours on the thinnest news. I thought of them as Beckett's Vladimir and Estragon:

Vladimir: Let's wait and see what he says.
Estragon: Who?
Vladimir: Godot.
Estragon: Good idea.
Vladimir: Let's wait till we know exactly how we stand.
Estragon: On the other hand it might be better to strike the iron before it freezes.
Vladimir: I'm curious to hear what he has to offer. Then we'll take it or leave it.
Estragon: What exactly did we ask him for?
Vladimir: Were you not there?
Estragon: I can't have been listening.
Vladimir: Oh . . . nothing very definite.

And nothing very definite was what we got. The first results were due at midday on Saturday. These were postponed until two o'clock. Then till four o'clock. Then we were told that in most places counting hadn't actually started because the counters were still being trained . . . because the ballot boxes hadn't arrived . . . because nobody had turned up to count . . . because reconciliation, whatever that was, couldn't be achieved. At first we smiled at the bumbling. Then we laughed at the extraordinary ineptitude. And then we knew that we were living in days of high farce.

The soon-to-be president warned of a disaster.

The electoral commission's judge lost his temper at a press briefing.

The next day the Judge apologized.

Radio commentators called the counting a débâcle.

The Judge said, 'You can't work in a brothel and remain chaste.'

There was much debate on whether the election was free and fair.

The Judge said the elections were a shambles.

The Judge said what did it matter.

The Judge said at least twenty million people had had their say.

Yes, it was free but not fair.

Yes, it was fair but not free.

According to one. According to another.

I do know that we heard some wonderful stories in those days. Stories about ballot boxes stuffed with grass. Stories about ballot boxes where all the papers were neatly stacked and all the crosses were for the beaming Buthelezi. Stories about warehouses full of ballot papers. Stories of boxes of ballot papers found on the tidelines of desolate beaches. Stories of computer freaks who hacked into the Independent Electoral Commission's data and changed the records. But the best story of all was the story of Nomaza Paintin.

Nomaza Paintin had been the first person to vote. Because she lived in New Zealand she went to cast her vote while we were still asleep. When we woke on Tuesday morning 26 April – the day designated for overseas and special votes – hers was the excited voice we heard on the radio proclaiming the joy of being the first black person to vote in South Africa's first democratic elections. And what's more she was a niece of the president-to-be. She said her vote represented the triumph of justice over oppression. She said her vote was for her uncle. She stood there dressed in the colours of the ANC and gave a clenched-fist salute and smiled for the television cameras before she entered the election booth. We heard her story again and again throughout the day. It was such a good story; it was so appropriate.

And then we heard that she wasn't a South African at all, that she had been born in Zimbabwe, and had never lived in South Africa. And then we heard that she was only distantly related to Nelson Mandela.

And then.

And then it came out that she was a friend of Joan Bolger, the wife of New Zealand's Prime Minister, Jim Bolger. In tears she had phoned her friend Joan on the Monday to say that it looked as if she wouldn't be able to vote. Probably Joan asked why, probably Nomaza told her that she no longer had valid papers, that after all she had been out of South Africa for so long. Probably Joan comforted her by saying she'd see what could be done.

Which was why later that day Nomaza received a telephone call from Naude Steyn, South Africa's ambassador to Australia. He said he'd spoken to the Judge at the IEC and the Judge had said it was all right, let her vote. The Judge had said something like this: If she's got the right documents that's fine, if she hasn't then mark the envelope invalid but let her go through the motions anyhow.

And so the first vote which counted for so much symbolically was invalid and no one knows if Nomaza knew or cared about the lie.

The Judge has said that the whole thing is a mere 'storm in a glass of water'. I think it is a typical story of this country. It is funny in one way, but in another it cuts right through to the rawness. I think it shows how deeply emotions run about the evils that were practised here. I think it also shows how we lie to one another. We lie to accommodate. We lie because we believe it does not matter. We lie because we think that in the face of so many years of misery, a lie that is for the good is not a lie at all. And we lie because we have no self-respect. We lie because we are victims. We lie because we cannot imagine ourselves in any other way.

There is Norman, for instance; he considers himself one of the victims.

On Wednesday 2 March 1994 Norman came to ask for money: I know which day it was because it is noted on the counterfoil in my chequebook. Perhaps 'ask' is not the right word, perhaps 'beg' is better. 'Ask' implies some dignity whereas there was nothing dignified about Norman. What he did was calculated and cynical and came from years of practice. What he did was charged with a history of apartheid, and the dying remnants of my guilt, and the complexity of relationships between haves and have-nots, and the fact that I was sitting there eating croissants and coffee. However, he also had been forced to beg for money because the country was economically stagnant.

He would not sit down. He would not have a cup of coffee. He stood, literally with his hat in his hand, his long face mournfully composed, and began: 'Mister Mike . . .'

Norman has not always called me Mister Mike. He used to call me Mike and we'd enjoyed some long conversations staring over the sea while he reminisced about his young trumpet-playing days in the bars and dives of the city. He told me he once earned a living by playing the trumpet but that he didn't play it much any more. He was sad about that. He hoped that maybe he'd be invited to join a band again some day. When I met him he was doing odd jobs: bricklaying, plastering, painting, nothing too consistent. As he described it he would earn enough to keep going for a while and then he'd sit in the sun or cycle around stopping off to chat whenever the fancy took him. And it took him frequently. In all those years I never learned if Norman was married or had children and it never occurred to me to ask.

Then came the day we decided to brick-pave our small back yard. I asked Norman if he would like the job and he took it, quoting a ridiculously low price. I ended up paying him a lot more but I had expected that would happen. It was during this job that he started calling me Mister Mike. I retaliated by calling him Mister Norman but the sarcasm was useless. He felt he had to extort money from me and he could only do that if I was put back in the position of the white boss and he took the subservient position of the cringing hard-done-by worker.

Since then I have remained Mister Mike.

And so now he stood in front of me and said: 'Mister Mike, times are really bad. I've cycled all the way to Constantia this morning to see about a job but now they want to wait until after the election and I've only got another job starting on Saturday. You see what am I supposed to do? When a man's got nothing what is he supposed to do? My little girl she says to me this morning, Daddy can't we have some chops tonight? She has to go to school without even a cup of tea in the morning. That's not right, Mister Mike. It's not right that little children should go hungry. When she says these things it stabs right at my heart, right in there, and I've got to say to her that it's all right that I'll get some money and we'll have food tonight. I can't say chops because chops is expensive but maybe some nice pilchards. And now what am I supposed to do, Mister Mike? I've cycled all the way to Constantia but they want to wait until after the election. I mean a man can go and steal and become a criminal but that's not right. I've been to jail. I know what it's like there in Pollsmoor. You know what I mean, Mister Mike? That's not a place for decent people. No, Mister Mike, a man can only ask when he's got no other way. If it was just me I wouldn't do it, but it's for the little girl, Mister Mike. Just some groceries. Some sugar and some flour. A man can only ask. These are bad times, you know what I mean. Everybody's waiting. And me myself I'm going to vote for the National Party. I mean what have they done to me. This country wouldn't be like this today without them. Just look at Africa, it's a mess. And then just look what we've got. The ANC's going to take all our houses away, Mister Mike. All we've worked for they're going to take. The blacks don't like the coloureds, it's a fact. Aren't you worried about what's going to happen?'

I told him I was not and hurriedly wrote out a cash cheque because I wanted him out of the house, I wanted him to stop his wheedling and his cultivated subservience, and I did not want to hear any more of his distorted rationalizations, but mostly I wanted to stop feeling so awful. And the only way I could do that was to get rid of Norman.

As I gave him the cheque I smelled liquor faintly on his breath. I had never seen him drunk; I had never seen him smoked up with dagga, and until that moment I had not thought he wanted the money for drink.

Norman knew what I was thinking.

'I'll bring you back the groceries so you can see I'm telling the truth,' he said quickly.

He understood the game. He had made it up; he had decided on the rules. 'I don't want it for drink or dagga.'

'I believe you,' I said, hating myself for saying it and knowing that I had fallen into the old vocabulary that kept us trapped within our roles. Yet part of Norman's fear was that he did not want anything to change. Because change would leave him an anachronism and his hard yet easy way of life would be jeopardized.

'I'll pay you back on Saturday. I promise, Mister Mike,' he said as he left. We both knew he was lying.

Two weeks later, on Wednesday 16 March 1994, he came to borrow more money. Once again I have the cheque counterfoil to remind me. Again it was midday

36

when he called but this time I wasn't eating. He knocked and I opened.

'Howzit Mister Mike,' he said, nodding to emphasize his greeting. 'Listen Mister Mike I've come to say I can pay you back on Saturday because I don't want to have to hide from you. Like I say I've got a job to build a wall for Mr Groenewald there in Plumstead, and when he pays me then I'll come straight down and pay you back.'

He stopped to assess how I was taking this.

'OK.' I smiled.

'Ah Mister Mike, can I have some more money just to get me through to Saturday? For groceries. For my little girl.'

I could not believe it. The audacity was numbing. But how could anybody, unless he was absolutely desperate, act like this? I wrote him out another cheque. And for it I got a complicated story as he probed to see if he could write off the debt by giving me a large packet of dagga.

'You know just up there at Lakeside,' he began, 'there near the post office. I was riding past there the other day when I hear the police sirens going and I look back and I see they're chasing this white Cortina towards me. There's two guys in the Cortina and just up ahead of me they throw a package into the grass which the police don't see. They keep on chasing the Cortina up the road. But I stopped and had a look at this package and its dagga, good dagga. Mister Mike, I haven't seen good dagga like that in a long time. But what's the good of it to me? I don't smoke. I won't say I didn't smoke when I was a lightie, but not any more now I'm a family man, you know what I mean! I suppose the best thing is just to burn it . . .'

He paused.

'I suppose so,' I said, feeling that for the first time I was part of the game.

'Ja well Mister Mike, see you, hey. Like I say I'll bring you the money on the weekend.'

He left and I have not seen him since. One day we will meet in the street and he will promise to pay me back on Saturday when he's paid for whatever job he will say he is doing. Of course he won't mean it so we will maintain the dishonesty between us; and his lies will sink through his life into the misery and unhappiness that he keeps suppressed beneath the drink and dagga.

Norman's story is so much like Nomaza's. So quintessential; so inescapable. So much a part of our lives where the facts and the fictions are confused. The point is that it has always been like this. Others have tried to see it simplistically: good against bad, black against white, system against struggle, and everything sanctified in the name of the cause. The cause that could condone killing and could inflict more suffering on those who already suffered unbearably. In the late Eighties, when North American companies were desperately disinvesting, I would listen to Archbishop Desmond Tutu calling for even harsher measures, stricter sanctions. I could only imagine that in the quiet of the night when he prayed to his God he prayed for the lives beneath the politics. I could only imagine that he prayed and wept, and must have felt lonely and afraid. Because how else could he have borne the knowledge of the small lives that were going hungry? The small lives that had lost their dignity. That had lost their children because they could no longer support them. What, I wondered, what about those often frightened, often bewildered people?

In 1988 I went to speak to some people at New Brighton, a township outside Port Elizabeth, who had lost their jobs when Ford and General Motors disinvested. I was researching an article for a magazine and I wanted to find out how sanctions were affecting those who really paid the price of politics. I had a contact called 'Benny' who had arranged the interview because in those days no one was talking. Fear was all-pervasive. Fear of the police. Fear of the comrades.

'You must understand,' Benny told me at his office in the city, 'that they might not want to talk to you, they might not want their names mentioned, and they might not want to have their photographs taken.'

I nodded.

'OK. You can leave your car here, mine's known in the township. We don't want to attract attention.'

It was a clear, winter's day in Port Elizabeth, but ten kilometres away at New Brighton where people did not have electricity the sky was hazy with smoke, the sun diffused and yellow. Those were tense days. The police and military patrolled the townships and there were radical factions within the community goading people to ever more extreme acts. Just three days before, a man had been necklaced in one of the major streets.

The men were waiting for us at Benny's house. There was Javu, bald and commanding. He was in his late fifties. And Timothy and Jacob, who were younger and reticent. We shook hands and I explained my purpose. They nodded and stressed that they did not want their names mentioned although they recanted on this a few days later.

Javu said, 'Just meeting you means they will call on us. They will want to know what you were doing here. Why we spoke to you.'

They, it was implied, were the police. But they could just as easily have been factions within the community.

Benny and Timothy lit cigarettes. It was tense, it was awkward. I was there to ferret around in their lives, touch raw nerves and watch the reaction. They were nervous, at first responding in monosyllables through Benny, who acted as interpreter. Then the frustration in Javu burst.

He railed in English against Ford for not letting the workers know they were pulling out, for not stifling the rumours and insecurity which had plagued them for months before the disinvestment; for reopening, via a management buy-out, as a new company, Delta, in Pretoria without offering anyone jobs there; for letting people know of the closure through mass-produced circulars instead of personally; for not paying adequate pensions; for not offering severance pay; and, most importantly, for not saying thank you for ten years of work.

The lack of thanks got to Javu the most, he kept coming back to it again and again.

Javu had not been laid off; he had resigned in solidarity with his fellow-workers because he 'wanted to keep my name clean'.

'December twelfth 1985 they pulled down the flags at the Neave factory. That was the last day for those chaps. And we all knew they were going to close the Cortina plant. I didn't want to work for these people so I resigned. The foreman he said to me, "But Javu, you're a good chap, you're a good man, why're you going?" I said no, I couldn't work for these people.'

I asked if he was married.

'Yes, I am married.'

'Any children?'

'Three daughters.'

'What did they think of your leaving?'

'I spoke to them. I told them what it was like at that place. They could see why I had to leave.'

'Have you tried to get another job?'

'Yes, I have tried, but who is going to employ an old man like me? They only think, But next year he turns sixty and then we have to pay him a pension. If Ford had paid me out I would have started my own business.'

'How much did Ford pay you?'

'A thousand rand.' (At the time worth about £250.)

'Was that pension money?'

'Yes. Only pension money.'

'What did you do with it?'

'I took that and I paid it on the furniture. I told them I have lost my job, I can't pay them any more, and they said, You've paid very well, you can pay us when you get money. Then I went to the rent office and I told them the same thing, and they said, That is all right you can pay us again when you get a job.'

'How do you get money for food and clothes?'

'My wife she works with a construction company.'

'Are you worried about not being the breadwinner?'

'Yes, it is not right. It is not right for a man. It is most hurtful.'

'Are you angry about what has happened?'

'Very angry.'

'Do you despair?'

'Yes, sometimes, but I have God. God is just. I pray to God and I know He will help us.'

'And what about the future? What are you going to do about the future?'

'I have hope. There is talk of a "package deal" from Ford. That money is my hope. That money and God.'

Javu smiled, a big smile he had used to emphasize his most telling points. It was a ready smile but his eyes stayed hard.

Sitting next to him was thirty-seven-year-old Timothy, who had smoked five cigarettes in an hour. He had been laid off in the middle of 1986 and lived now on his sister's

41

charity. She looked after his two children, she gave him food and, occasionally, money. Timothy said his wife could not find a job either.

Through Benny I asked him if he had any food in the house. He shook his head. Any tea, sugar, bread, jam? Again he shook his head. 'Ask him what he had for breakfast.'

'His sister gave him three pieces of bread last night and he kept one so that he could have it for breakfast this morning,' Benny translated.

'How does he cope with this?'

Benny relayed the question and for a moment a horrible mask of pain distorted Timothy's face, it looked as if he was about to cry. But he did not. He answered Benny who then said, 'Sometimes he locks himself in his room. He sits there in his room and cries.'

Benny did not like this; he, too, was smoking now almost from one cigarette to another. I did not like it either. I did not want to ask these questions and I did not want to hear the answers. I hated reporting. Yet some perverse side of me kept on and on.

Benny got up to ask his daughter to make tea and the tension eased slightly. When he returned I asked about Jacob, who had sat there quietly all this time fidgeting with his short beard.

He lived with his mother and two brothers. The elder one, Sandy, had tuberculosis and could not work. He used to get money from a government fund for the disabled but had not had anything since 1980. His younger brother, Connie, was an epileptic and could not work either. Until Ford disinvested, Jacob's wages were enough to feed the family and cover most of their expenses. But now the only money coming into the home was the meagre wage his mother earned as a domestic servant.

Jacob seldom smiled, his forehead was permanently creased in worry. He explained through Benny that he only ate one meal a day at supper. 'Sometimes that is soup, bread and coffee, sometimes it is just bread and coffee,' Benny relayed.

'Has he had any temporary jobs?'

'No,' Benny translated. 'But he looks for temporary jobs all the time.'

By early afternoon we all needed a break. I agreed to visit Javu in the evening, and then Benny and I spent some time drifting around the township. We visited the Ford plant to which these men had walked every morning for so many mornings of their lives. The buildings had been taken over by the Department of Education and Training and, judging by the security, the police.

The township streets were busy. On the corners women sold oranges, children played with a tricycle that had only two wheels, men sat in the sun or talked in groups in the small back yards. There were more men about than women. The women who passed us had a sense of purpose, seemed to be hurrying somewhere.

Often Benny stopped to talk to friends. He was well known. Sometimes he drew me into the conversations and I tried to get them to respond to questions on disinvestment. But they wouldn't. They looked at me with a smile and refused to say anything.

Always it was at this point that interest faded, the conversations became awkward, and Benny's friends switched into Xhosa. It was as if the word 'disinvestment' had become too politically loaded: they would not risk an opinion, nor even fall back on apartheid as the source of all evil.

We arrived at Javu's house at dusk. Before we went in Benny advised me not to mention the word disinvestment but to talk about 'when Ford pulled out'. He added that it was the same thing and maybe then they would talk.

I acquiesced. But wanted to know, why the semantics?

'Because', he explained with some exasperation, 'nobody's going to say anything that can be used to bash Tutu. Maybe they are victims, maybe they are suffering, but how can they trust you? How can they trust anyone? If the archbishop says sanctions are needed, they are not going to argue with him. At least not to you.'

Javu had new carpets in his lounge and dining room and they were covered in plastic runners for protection. The furniture too was new, the seats also encased in plastic. On a stand in the corner was a large-screen television, but the houses in this part of New Brighton did not have electricity. Usually he ran the television from a generator but that had been broken for some months.

I asked if he owed much on the television.

'No.' A big smile. 'We have paid for it out of my wife's salary.'

'And the carpets?'

'Another five hundred rand to pay.'

Daylight faded quickly from the room and his daughter placed paraffin lamps on the dining-room table and the top of the television set.

There was a knock on the door and a man in his early thirties was introduced. He agreed to be interviewed but I could not use his name.

'Yes,' interjected Javu, 'that's how it should be. Then it comes from the people.'

From where I was sitting the man's bearded face was in shadow, but sometimes while he talked I got the feeling he was close to tears, especially when his hands knotted one way and then another in his lap.

He had worked up through the ranks at Ford, starting as

44

a labourer and ending as a supervisor when he was laid off in June 1986. He had had very little money in the last two years.

'Sometimes we only have a hundred rand for food a month. That's bad. We must eat once a day in the evening. Every day I go looking for jobs. I walk to all the factories and I ask them for work. I ask them please haven't they got a job. I apply to the adverts but I've still got no job.'

On the spur of the moment I decided to ignore Benny's advice about using the word disinvestment. In my frustration I loaded the question: 'You're a victim, you've been hurt: do you think disinvestment's a good thing?'

There was a pause. The newcomer clicked his tongue, covered his mouth with his hand, laughed and looked away. 'Have you heard of the state of emergency?' he asked. That was the only answer I would get. It was the only answer any of them would give.

'You see,' explained Javu, not without a hint of triumph, 'we do not even discuss these things with our friends.' He was too polite to add, So why should we discuss them with you? But I got the picture.

It always came down to 'getting the picture'. Nothing was categorically stated, it was all implied. How were we ever going to solve this problem if they would not talk about it, I wanted to know?

There was no response except smiles. Perhaps it was fear, fear of everything: of police, of comrades, of betraying leaders they would not even admit they supported. Sometimes there also seemed to be an incomprehension, a sense that they did not understand why the politics had to be that way.

The next day I talked to Javu's wife Lilian on the construction site where she worked as a tea lady. She was fragile and small-boned. In a tiny room with a fridge, a basin and side-table where she made tea, she sat down, a

45

tissue twined through her fingers. She talked very softly and it did not take long for the tears to come. But, for a while, I persisted.

'You knew Javu was going to lose his job?'

She lifted her glasses and mopped at her eyes: 'Yes. He told me everything. I knew he was unhappy there.'

She was crying silently now, not trying to dry her eyes, the tears falling in her lap, on her coat, leaving damp patches that got bigger and bigger.

'What did you feel when he came home and said that's it, that he wasn't going back?'

'It didn't feel nice. I used to lie awake at night.'

'Did you have anyone to talk to?'

'No, no one.'

She wept.

There was nothing I could do. I tried to comfort her. I apologized. I stood around uselessly. Men in hard hats rushed past the door. She took them tea during the day. She had worked with most of them for five years. They probably knew nothing of her home life.

'Sorry I'm a cry baby,' she said. But she could not stop crying.

It was knocking-off time so I drove her home. In the car she said, 'I've got to work. I can't do otherwise. What would happen to my family?'

And then as I drove away from her house I saw Javu, who flagged me down.

'What did my wife say?' he wanted to know.

I told him she was very upset.

'Yes, but what did she say? Was it about me or Ford, or because of the money?'

He launched into a long story that eventually came to the point that all women wanted was money so that they could go shopping at the supermarkets, so that they could buy new dresses. But life was hard, he said, why didn't women understand that was the way of life?

'You know what I do. I'll tell you what I do. I play the horses. Every day there is races, Monday, Wednesday, Saturday I gamble on the horses. That is the way we live.'

I left Javu leaning on his gate, smiling and waving as I drove away. You learned a little bit new every time, I thought. Even when you did not want to.

I saw Javu again in the winter of 1994. Almost six years to the day had passed. He remembered the time before but now his political rhetoric was jubilant.

'At last this country is ours again,' he said. 'It was worth the suffering.'

'Was it?' I asked.

We were in his sitting room: the plastic runners still covered the carpets, but at some stage they had been stripped from the couch and the armrests showed the white fibres of the undercloth. An uncomfortably warm winter sun lay on the floor and on the chair where I sat. I squirmed in it, over-dressed for its heat. It was a Saturday afternoon and Javu had the television on to watch the horse races at Durban's Gosforth Park. He still had no electricity and the TV set was being powered by a twelve-volt battery.

He picked up on my question about the political sacrifice without hesitation.

'Of course,' he said.

'Being without a job and not having food?'

'We always had food.'

'Some people didn't,' I reminded him. 'Like Jacob next door.'

'I gave Jacob food. Maybe sometimes he was hungry but he never starved. There was always some food. Let me tell you, it was because of what we did that de Klerk had to change. If he hadn't changed there would have been big

47

trouble. But now it is good. We can vote. Mandela is president. My daughters will not know what it was like before. They will be proper people.'

For Javu and Lilian life was still 'hard', as he had once told me. In the last six years he had done piece-work in engineering workshops and with auto-repair garages, but nothing was permanent. The longest job lasted eight months. Lilian worked throughout at the construction company and for the last eighteen months had been working as a domestic on Saturdays for an extra R30. Javu still played the horses. He said he won more often than he lost and maybe he did but the horse he had backed, High Flier, lost the race we watched.

'Sometimes it happens like this,' he said with the nonchalance of the inured punter.

I asked him how much he had lost.

'Twenty bucks,' he said and smiled. 'I'll get it back. No problem.'

He looked no different to the man in the magazine photograph taken in 1988. He was still slim and strong-featured and his eyes had not tired. They were as direct as they had been before, almost challenging, unblinking. He brought out a quart bottle of beer and poured two tumblersful and told me about the six years. It was a description of life without, yet he was undaunted by it.

'No, I'm not bitter,' he said. 'We have struggled and we have triumphed. We have triumphed for all the people in the country. So why should I be bitter? We can drink beer here in the sun. Life is good, my friend.'

I left Javu soon after that. His next race was about to start and I did not want to see him lose all the money Lilian would earn that day. I did not want to see him win either. I wanted to end this story while I was ahead.

The first election results I heard gave the National Party the lead in the Western Cape. It was not entirely unexpected. In January, Jill had written up some research into coloured businesses in the greater Cape Town area that clearly showed that the coming day of liberation was being viewed with apprehension.

She reported that many businesspeople saw the uncertain political climate as an obstacle to economic growth. She wrote that many

> were adopting a wait-and-see attitude to the forthcoming election but nowhere did there seem to be an overt optimism now that the era of legislated apartheid was ending. The current violence, particularly in the black townships, was said to be hampering business and opportunities for growth. One supermarket, for example, had been bombed within weeks of starting up and had lost valuable equipment. The taxi war was also affecting business as customers avoided the more volatile area where many of these businesses were situated.

Given this, given Norman's opinions, given the lipstick-smeared posters of F. W. de Klerk adorning the walls of some local factories where the workforce was largely made up of coloured people, it would have been a surprise if the results had turned out otherwise. In the end, common blood, the Afrikaans language, religion, conservatism, fear, made many residents in Mitchells Plain, Mannenberg, Retreat, Bontheuwel, Grassy Park and the other suburbs of Cape Town, and beyond in the dorps and on the farms, rise and vote for the NP. Vote even for those men who short years before had denied them access to a decent education, public amenities, to human dignity. It was an object lesson in history and politics. It showed the weakness of the former and the expediency of the latter. As

Norman had said, 'The blacks don't like the coloureds, it's a fact.'

For the *Cape Times'* columnist Sandile Dikeni the ANC's defeat was bitter news. 'The culture of slavery which began in the Cape for South Africa will not be gone until the chains are thrown into the sea,' he wrote.

> With all respect for the National Party victory in our province, Hernus Kriel [former minister of police, now premier of the Western Province] shall never, in my opinion, be seen as a liberator. That is the truth blowing in the South-Easter, especially from the side of Khayelitsha where the heavy sounds of defeat ricochet from the corrugated iron dwellings we still live in.

If the Western Cape result was not entirely unexpected, then neither were the results elsewhere as they slowly, almost hesitantly, came in. And so the ANC decisively took seven of the nine regions. Except that no one had expected them to lose by quite such a margin in kwaZulu/Natal, where Inkatha received fifty per cent of the vote to the ANC's thirty-two per cent. And no one expected Inkatha to get anywhere near ten per cent nationally. Some polls conducted in Natal were almost one hundred per cent inaccurate. Or rather, the figures were correct, it was just that they were attributed to the wrong parties. Nevertheless, it gave pause to wonder how a political party that up to a week before 27 April was intent on boycotting the election could mobilize such large support throughout rural kwaZulu/Natal so effectively.

By late Monday we were getting tired of the Judge's incompetencies. His IEC was blundering hopelessly. What had been funny was now becoming tedious. Everyone wanted to get on. Everyone knew what the result would be. Yet there was still less than half the vote counted and the job that should have been finished by Sunday night now did not look as if it was ever going to end. The politicians were edgy. They wanted to celebrate, because few were going to mourn the results of this election. On Radio Metro Tim Modise said, 'This is not going to be a victory of blacks over whites. This is where we all win. Blacks and whites and coloureds and Indians together.' And people – blacks, whites, coloureds, Indians – phoned him to say yes, brother, this was for everybody.

On Monday afternoon de Klerk conceded defeat. He stood before his supporters at the National Party headquarters in Pretoria and with his eyes brimming he bade them goodbye. Later he told a television reporter: 'Mr Mandela deserves the congratulations, good wishes and prayers of all South Africa. I hold out my hand to him in friendship and co-operation. Our greatest task will be to ensure that our young and vulnerable democracy takes root and flourishes.'

The next day the ANC held street parties in Johannesburg and at the city's Carlton Hotel. And for the first time Nelson Mandela cried in public. He was cheered and adored and he shed tears. And we shed tears with him.

'People of South Africa,' he called out, 'this is a joyous night. I look forward to working with you for our beloved country.'

I still do not know if there was ever a final tally. There must have been. Surely there must have been. I do recall the Judge releasing figures on the Friday, which may be how I know that the ANC got sixty-two per cent, the NP twenty per cent, Inkatha ten per cent, the Freedom Party two per cent, and the Democratic Party and the Pan

Africanist Congress such insignificant percentages that they only have seven and five seats in Parliament respectively. But by then, of course, the results no longer mattered.

3

Celebration and euphoria were much in the air during May and June. Even the storms of June did little to dispel the ardour with which we cherished our moment. It was then my thoughts turned to Emma and Howard, and I wondered if they would not provide an exemplary story of what people were calling 'our new South Africa'.

I first met Emma and Howard in August 1989 when I interviewed them for an Italian magazine that wanted an article on 'love across the colour bar'. At the time they had been pessimistic, despairing; now I expected their world would have changed utterly. It had, but not as I had anticipated. Instead I was told a curious story of love and defiance and disillusionment.

Howard and Emma have a difficult relationship. Two years after their marriage they were divorced and they have not remarried. They live together, and have two children, and Emma is pregnant again. But it has not been easy. They have sometimes broken apart, swearing to go their separate ways, but their ways have always converged again.

In South African racial parlance Howard and Emma are known as a 'mixed couple'. Howard is coloured, Emma is white. Ten years ago their love affair was illegal and they had to hide from the police. When I saw them in 1989 the

Immorality Act had been taken off the statute book but they could still not legally live together. Nor could Emma legally live with her daughter Taryn, who was classified coloured. However, the Group Areas Act was not being rigorously enforced and they had managed to rent a flat in Claremont, a white suburb of Cape Town. They were in their mid-twenties. They knew that they lived in the flat by the good grace of their neighbours.

This is the story they told me then. It is well to remember how things were just a few years ago and what this has done to us.

EMMA: I hate the set-up. One of our neighbours just has to say something and we can be evicted at any time. This thought is always present. There was an incident the other morning: I went into the bathroom to see two white hands at the top of the window. Somebody had been looking over. I got such a fright. At first I thought it was just a peeping Tom, but Howard said maybe it was one of the right-wing radicals.

On another occasion a social welfare officer came round because they'd had reports that I beat up my daughter and that I was living with a coloured man who beat me up. Fortunately I work at a crèche which is attached to a social welfare organization so I could refer this officer to my director and the file was closed. But we both know that someone was trying to intimidate us.

This sort of thing happens all the time. Just the other day the estate agent for the block of flats came to ask me if I was having political meetings here. Someone had told him that lots of blacks and coloured people came to see me and he automatically assumed we were politically active. He couldn't believe they were just my friends and left warning me to be careful.

HOWARD: I find it terribly strange to say I'm married and we're a mixed couple, so I try to keep quiet about it at work. At a job interview I'd never mention that I was married across the colour bar because it would spoil my chances of getting the job. My current employer knows about it and I don't think he likes it but it hasn't changed his attitude towards me.

I would say that mixed couples have terrible strains in their relationships, just coping with apartheid. Just coping with being a mixed couple. In the early days when we were going out, people used to look at us in the street and I'd be conscious of it. I used to turn around to see if people were looking at us. I don't do that any more. People still look at us but it doesn't bother me any more.

But as Emma says, there is this feeling we're being spied on all the time, that we're different, and we're a challenge to white people. When the welfare officer called about Taryn I felt very angry. It's bad, it hurts, but there's nothing you can do about it. And just the fact that there's nothing you can do about it makes you even more angry, and there's no one to take it out on so then we fight. I get so upset that I fight with Emma.

EMMA: I would say apartheid was a major reason for our divorce. It wasn't the only reason; we also had other personal problems like all couples. But when you've got to cope with this thing – this situation – on top of that it makes it very difficult. It means you've got to try a lot harder. Which is what we're doing now.

I don't think either of us have ever thought that we're making love across the colour bar. When you love some-body you love them for what they are. You don't think about things like that. I didn't think of Howard as a coloured. You don't. When you're friends with someone you don't see the colour of their skin. They're friends, or lovers, you don't see them as being coloured, or black, or white.

When I told my father – my mother died when I was eight years old – about Howard he accepted it. He respects my decisions. He's never said anything against Howard.

Me having a coloured boyfriend wasn't a big thing for my white friends either. After I left school I did an apprenticeship to become a hairdresser. I became friendly with a coloured girl on the course. I slept over at her house one night and the next afternoon we were walking through the neighbourhood when some boys called us in to have a drink. We did, and that was where I met Howard.

HOWARD: I remember it was the end of our technical training and we were having a party to celebrate. I suppose we'd had a few too many so when we saw these girls in the street we asked them in.

We were laughing and fooling around, you know how it is, and then eventually Emma and I started talking and we liked each other so we started going out.

Of course in those days – it was 1983 – it was heavy, so we had to be careful. But in the coloured area it was easier and we were usually with other mixed couples so it wasn't too bad. I can't even remember what our first date was like; it was probably at a party with my friends so we wouldn't have been too worried.

Only once were we approached by the police. We were having a braai in the forest with some other mixed couples when a police patrol drove up. They asked a few questions and warned us that we were breaking the law but that was all. Sure it was unpleasant. That sort of thing's not nice, it hurts, it makes you angry, but there's nothing you can do about it. So you just keep it all bottled up inside you.

Socially our friends have never mixed, either we go into my world or we go into Emma's world. It's as if they can't mix because they are from such different worlds, they do different things, they even think differently. This puts a tremendous strain on a relationship. I think we spend most of our time with my family and friends.

EMMA: My white friends don't mind. It's not a problem to them. But we don't see very much of them any more.

It's much easier to live among coloured people because once they've satisfied their curiosity they accept you as normal people. White people watch us all the time, waiting for signs of strain, waiting to be reassured that what we're doing is not right. As a result we spend most of our social life 'that side' with Howard's family and friends.

I remember when we decided to get divorced in 1987 my family said it was inevitable. And still, just the other day, my father asked me if I didn't marry Howard to get some sort of revenge on him. Not that he doesn't like Howard, he really does, but . . .

HOWARD: But there will always be something between us.

EMMA: I'm worried about the future. When I hear about the Conservative Party I wonder, if they came to power, would they put coloured people into homelands and what would happen to our family. Where do we go? Can it happen? I don't know which way the country's going politically, so I just ignore these issues. The fight's going out of all of us now. In 1985 when the Immorality Act and the Mixed Marriages Act were scrapped so that we could legally get married, we really thought things were going to change. We knew there was still the Group Areas Act, but we thought that maybe that would be scrapped soon as well. But it hasn't been. And it's so stupid. It makes me so angry that they don't get rid of that law so that we can live like ordinary people. For instance, down the road is a school that would be ideal for Taryn. But it's a government school for whites only and Taryn is registered as coloured. There are no coloured junior schools in the area, our only option is to send her to a private school, but that is very expensive. So you see there are so many dead ends. But we live constantly in the hope that something's going to happen. Yet when I really start thinking about it, the situation seems so helpless that I blot it out. I don't want to think about it.

HOWARD: It took four years to establish apartheid; it's going to take four thousand years to demolish it. What we've got to do is sort out our lives, make ourselves strong and leave the authorities to their childish laws. Obviously they will impose on us, but we must turn our backs against that because the system will continue for a long while yet. There's no way the Afrikaners are going to give power to blacks. They are so strong. They've got control of everybody, irrespective of who you are. They've been controlling this country for years, there's no way they can be overthrown.

What we really want is to have a house of our own in a suburb where we'd like to live. And for there to be no more Group Areas Act, no more apartheid.

And it's the same for Taryn. We don't want her to have to go through the hurt, the anger and the frustration that we've had to – and still have to – live with.

I met Emma and Howard again in Theresa's Restaurant in Muizenberg because over the telephone Howard told me they did not want to be interviewed at their home. Let's go to a pub and have some beers, he had said.

The way I remembered Howard and Emma was wrong. I had thought he was shorter and gaunt, and she plump, whereas she was thin, almost scrawny. And Howard was round-faced, tall and well-fleshed. He was more confident than the previous time. He talked emphatically; he gestured when he made remarks he felt deeply about. Also he was relaxed: his hands lay calmly on the table beside his glass of beer or he leaned back in the chair and watched me. In 1989 I remember he would not look me in the eye and had sat rigidly throughout the interview. Emma was still thoughtful, articulate, aware of where she was and what was happening. She was probably aware that what she called 'our plans for the future' offered no solution, but I do not think she wanted to acknowledge this. She was trying to convince herself that leaving the country would give them the chance they had not had before. Howard, however, was convinced their plans would bring peace to their world.

They still did not have Howard's dream house in the suburbs. What they had was a 'separate entrance', a common enough situation: a double garage that had been converted into a small flat. It was one of a number of dwellings on a suburban plot.

EMMA: We're living in a coloured area and it has actually brought out the differences in our upbringings. Things that are unacceptable to me are perfectly normal in this environment. It is perfectly normal for women to be considered second-rate citizens. They must cook and clean and be satisfied with whatever their husbands do or say. It drives me insane. It makes me so angry. I feel what I do is important and I don't expect to be treated like a dishcloth. Living in a coloured area has been more tempting for Howard. All his buddies come round and say, Don't let your wife henpeck you. So that has been a new pressure. Women are just expected to sit at home and look after babies. It's a common factor in this environment. In a way statute racism was easier to handle, because it was a law and we were going against the grain so it was real and I could accept it. But this is something that has no outside excuse. It's something that becomes very personal and you can't excuse it.

It makes me feel very isolated. I've noticed that if we're sitting in a group people will go and sit everywhere else but next to me. I feel like an alien. I suppose it has always been like this but before we used to socialize with mixed couples so it wasn't so obvious.

HOWARD: I don't think there has ever been the slightest bit of racism in me. As a kid maybe. Then very much. I can remember as a teenager I felt so much anger. I remember one day we were invited to a party in Claremont. Our teacher – she was a white girl – she had a party at her home and invited us. I think I must have been about sixteen. It was at the time of the boycotts and riots and everybody had heavy feelings. You just had to be white and say something and I would go for you. Everything was going fine at the party until this white guy got drunk and started making racial insults. I just went for him, hit him, tore his clothes off him. I can actually see it very clearly how I started hitting him. I remember having this guy on the top of my shoulders and wanting to throw him down the stairs and see him fall. That's all I wanted to do. I just wanted to see him fall. But eventually my friends calmed me down and he went home. When I look back at it I get scared because of that rage. I remember going to a coloured nightclub in Salt River where they had white bouncers. And there was this whitey telling me what to do. I was prepared to take on all five bouncers. This anger actually makes me scared. And it's all because of the problem with race.

I think I've got to a stage where all I want to see is my

family grow up. We started at A and built ourselves up and then we slipped back and now it's up to me to build us up again. And I'm determined to do that. I've just got to a stage where I'm more mature. I still want a nice home.

But for a couple of months now I've had this feeling that I don't want to live in South Africa any more. I want to go and live in Swaziland or somewhere. In Africa but . . .

EMMA: I think an important factor in our relationship is that my family put unrealistic expectations on us. Taryn has had to suffer for this. She has recently had to go to Square Hill Primary School, which is a good couple of degrees below what she had. What she had we conned our way through. We couldn't afford the fees or the uniforms but we somehow managed to get her through. Then we got to the stage after our last separation where we realized we could only give what we could afford. It has affected her quite badly. She deserves a lot more. I have just begun to feel that we don't have much to offer her here in South Africa. Things are changing but still the two of us can't afford to keep her in a decent school. We've accepted the fact that if we stay in South Africa we're going to give our kids second-best.

HOWARD: Blacks outnumber all the other population groups totally in this country. We're outnumbered. These people have been oppressed for umpteen years. I'm not saying that they're cramping my lifestyle by coming up and saying, 'Here we are, we've been oppressed for all these years, now we need the breaks, we need the jobs, we need the houses, we need everything.' I mean coloured people lived in luxury compared to how those people have suffered all these years. I am prepared to give it all up for them. That's the way I feel. I feel that I don't stand a chance here. I'm in a good trade. I'm an auto-electrician. In the whole of South Africa there's only two and a half thousand qualified auto-electricians. It's a complicated job, but I feel the whole job market, the housing market, is going to be overwhelmed by blacks. I'm not saying this because I'm racist. What's happening is because of damage that's been done years and years ago. The thing that makes me sick is, the people who caused it are not suffering. They're not going to suffer. But they should be taken out and hung.

EMMA: Even de Klerk?

HOWARD: He should be hung.

EMMA: But look what the man did.

HOWARD: He should be hung.

EMMA: But he did it out of a sense of what was right.

HOWARD: He had to do it.

EMMA: He didn't have to let Mandela out of jail.

HOWARD: And live in a country that had no money left!

They were both silent for a long time and then Howard asked: Why did there ever have to be something such as white and black? I need somebody to answer that question. Why? I need an answer. Until I get an answer the only people I'm going to look out for are my family. The days of fighting for the coloured community are over. It doesn't work. This scar above my eye is from where a policeman hit me with a baton at a protest march. It's over. It's just for my family now.

He finished his beer.

It's going to be the coloured people who suffer. Already there's job reservation. Soon there's going to be coloured people walking the street looking for jobs. We're going to have laws saying that jobs must go to black people first. I know I'm going to suffer, which doesn't make me angry towards the black people. I'm going to step away and give them the space. We didn't suffer. I'm not going to say I'm free at last. We lived in houses. They lived in shacks. I think the blacks have gone through this change very peacefully. I mean the violence that happened here was only the tip of the iceberg compared to what should have happened.

EMMA: The reason I would like to leave is that our relationship has lasted ten years and during those ten years we've moved from white to coloured areas. We've tried this and tried that and there has always been some sort of trauma. In a normal marriage you experience problems but with us they are emphasized. I've got to the stage where I'm tired of it. I would like to go to a country where you are accepted for what you are. I don't want Taryn to come home and tell me they're calling her 'milkybar'. That poor kid. It's been a big culture shock for her to go to a coloured school and I feel guilty. And then I feel guilty for feeling guilty.

She says to me, 'Mommy, I don't like this school. The kids swear and they smoke and they touch my bum.' These are things she never experienced before. She had Boesak [Allan, formerly a priest, but during the election the ANC's candidate for premier of the Western Province] at her school telling them to give the black-power salute and shout Boe-sak, Boe-sak, Boe-sak. And her teacher telling her that I must vote ANC. That's heavy. She's got pressures on her she doesn't need.

We want to set down roots. We've never been able to set down roots.

HOWARD: We've always had friends going to Australia or wherever. But we've always said no, we'll stay here and fight this thing out. And now look, the country's changed, but not for us. Know what I mean? Things won't come right in our generation. The country's fucked. I'm sorry to use that word but the country's fucked. And the only time it will come right will be with our kids. Race won't be an issue to them.

EMMA: I'm glad things have worked out the way they have. I think the country is going to change and for the better. It's just that our lives have been messed up. I would like to go to a country where things are normal and where you know what to expect next.

HOWARD: I don't think we can bear living with this country as it goes through the changes. It might sound defeatist. But it's going to kill us.

EMMA: I need some tranquillity and peace.

HOWARD: We'll go next year.

EMMA: We have lost hope. I believe in Taryn. She's lost so much.

HOWARD: I've got this perception of our children becoming perfect citizens where there's no race, none of the bad side of life. They must be happy people, but it is so difficult teaching that to a child in this country.

EMMA: We're not going to fit in here. And now I see it happening to Taryn. It hurts worse when you see it happening to a child.

As we left the restaurant Emma said, 'Well, I suppose you got more than you bargained for!'

'I suppose so.' I agreed, feeling a mixture of emotions that included disappointment, and a sadness about them, and a realization that I had been given yet another lesson in the ordinary complexity of people's lives.

'Tell me one last thing,' I asked as we were about to part. 'What did the election mean for you?'

Howard answered first, quickly, speaking ahead of his thoughts: 'It was great. Although to be quite honest with you I was very confused about what party to vote for.'

'In the beginning you were totally National Party,' Emma interjected.

'Yes,' Howard admitted as if this was a reluctant

confession. Then he faced up to it: 'As Emma says, I was totally National Party. But I stood in the polling queue and started thinking back and I thought: Me, vote for these NP bastards that have caused all this *kak* in my life? I'm going to go for the ANC. So I voted ANC. I've never been politically involved in any party but that day I thought, Let's make a change here.'

'I was stunned when you came home and told me because you were so Nat,' said Emma.

Howard laughed.

'I felt good afterwards. I felt good. I felt good when they had the party at the Carlton Hotel and Mandela stood there and he cried. That's when I felt good. We've got a lovely photograph of Mandela in our lounge. He's a remarkable man. A very good man.'

'He is,' said Emma. 'I trust Mandela. I believe in him. But I am very unsure about the party. They promised so much. Both the ANC and the Nats were promising so much that in all good conscience I couldn't vote. I didn't know who to believe. But Mandela's an honest man.'

4

When I recall the day of Mandela's inauguration, what I remember first is the emotion. I remember listening to Radio Metro in the afternoon when the ceremony was over and being unable to stop the prickling behind my eyes as one person after another phoned the station to express the feelings they wanted so desperately to share. Their voices were almost inchoate with sentiment. They said it was wonderful. They said it was magnificent. They said Nelson Mandela was the most remarkable man. They said that for the first time in their days they were glad to be alive in this place. I knew what they meant. I blinked to keep away the tears but I could not. I stood in the back yard and looked up at the mountain and listened to their voices and the voice of the DJ that was as broken as those of the callers, and I knew what they meant. I had never expected to feel this way about this people and this country.

That evening Catherine phoned to say the emotion was flooding her. Catherine is French. She came to South Africa almost two decades ago and her first experience of the country was to be tear-gassed while the police stormed an anti-apartheid demonstration in the centre of Cape Town. Now she said, 'This is a moment greater than anything I felt in France at the end of the Sixties. I am glad I'm here.'

She had video-taped the entire inauguration proceedings and was sitting with a glass of wine going through it all over again. 'It is extraordinary,' she said. 'Extraordinary that there should be a man like this here now. When he stood up to read his speech and he took his glasses out of his jacket pocket, I cried. That simple gesture. It seemed to carry everything he has been through in his life.'

I have heard so many stories of how people celebrated that day. Some have said they danced. Some have said they sang. Some opened champagne. Some sat quietly, partly in mourning for what it had cost to reach this moment, partly because what was happening was so profound that the occasion was greater than language. These were private celebrations where people needed the solace of being alone to participate in the day.

The day was 10 May 1994. In Pretoria, on the lawns before the Union Buildings, thousands of people gathered to witness the inauguration of President Nelson Mandela. There were six thousand foreign and local dignitaries. Among them, PLO leader Yasser Arafat; Israel's President Ezer Weizman; Cuba's President Fidel Castro; Tanzanian founding president Julius Nyerere; Benazir Bhutto, Prime Minister of Pakistan; Al Gore, Vice President of the USA; Hillary Clinton; Douglas Hurd, the British Foreign Secretary; Prince Philip; the list was long and impressive.

As he came in Castro said, 'It is a historic day. I am pleased to be here. I wish you peace, harmony and unity for the great task ahead of you.'

Eighteen years earlier he had had to send his soldiers to help the embattled Angolan regime stop the South African troops invading that country.

All through the morning the dignitaries arrived. The radio commentators discussed what these people wore and who they were. They commented on the strange crown-like hat Winnie Mandela was wearing; and on the pith helmet Marika de Klerk thought appropriate. They discussed saris and military uniforms; they drew attention to former arch-enemies who now sat beside one another; and to current arch-enemies who now sat beside one another. They pointed out James Gregory, who for a quarter of a century had been Mandela's jail warden. Both he and his wife had been flown to Pretoria at the president's request. They remarked on what a grand occasion this was.

At twelve-thirty the Deputy Presidents were sworn in. F. W. de Klerk swore on the Holy Trinity; Thabo Mbeki said, 'So help me God.' They made their speeches; they promised their allegiance.

Ten minutes later the Chief Justice called the President. Nelson Mandela stood up and the crowd rose to receive him. I wondered at the self-control with which he faced such moments. I thought it was probably the Island still in him. The Chief Justice read the oath, and the President said, 'So help me God.'

He was given his speech and took out his glasses from a pocket inside his jacket. He put them on. He glanced at the assembly; he looked down at the paper.

I thought: This would not have been the same without him. The prisoner became the president. We needed what he had strived for, what he had been jailed for, what he had been freed for. We needed all our history symbolized in one person.

Mandela read, 'Today, all of us do, by our presence here, and by our celebrations in other parts of our country and the world, confer glory and hope to newborn liberty.'

He said, 'The time for the healing of wounds has come.

The moment to bridge the chasms that divide us has come. The time to build is upon us.'

He said, 'We understand it still that there is no easy road to freedom. We know it well that none of us acting alone can achieve success. We must act together as a united people, for national reconciliation, for nation-building, for the birth of a new world. Let there be justice for all. Let there be peace for all. Let there be work, bread, water and salt for all.

'Let each know that for each the body, the mind and the soul have been freed to fulfil themselves.

'Never, never and never again shall it be that this beautiful land will again experience the oppression of one by another and suffer the indignity of being the skunk of the world.

'Let freedom reign.

'The sun shall never set on so glorious a human achievement!

'God bless Africa!

'I thank you.'

He said those last three words deliberately, carefully, slowly. He ends all his speeches with them. And there is something in the cadence that makes me shiver every time I hear them. Because in them is twenty-seven years of imprisonment. In them is the winter wind that comes off the sea and scours over Robben Island and eats into the soul the way salt pits iron. In them is the measure of hope overcoming despair.

As Mandela sat down, to the applause, the shouts, the ululation, so the oral poet Mzwakhe Mbuli began to declaim:

'Let me dedicate my poetic praises to the symbol of
   resistance

Let me dedicate my poetic praises to the symbol of hope
    and inspiration
Let me dedicate my poetic praises to the fountain of
    wisdom and inspiration
I talk of Nelson Rolihlahla Madiba Mandela
I talk of Nelson Madiba
I talk of a leader like a golden diamond
I talk of a leader like diamonds and gold
You have gone through the fires of time in order to be
    refined
You have gone through all forms of life
I talk of Nelson Rolihlahla Mandela
Like an oak tree you have survived all kinds of weather
Comrade Mandela, you are a hero, you are a veteran,
You are a stalwart, you are a catalyst to unite,
You are the father of a new nation in the making.'

But perhaps what was to come next was to signify most
clearly what had changed. For out of the south came a
formation of planes that rocked in their flight and their
engine noise filled the sky. And behind them came jets that
released trails of smoke: black, green, red, white. And
behind them came helicopter gunships flying the new flag
from their undercarriages.

Which was when people raised their arms and began to
shout: 'They are our planes now. They are our planes
now.'

And a woman broke down in tears and said, 'Those
planes killed my son. But now they belong to us. They
belong to the people.'

It was a day I could not have imagined. And particularly I
could not have imagined the high emotion. Yet like so
many I knew the day would come.

In 1976 I felt its imminence for the first time, and for the first time in my life was aware of the stirring of history. This manifested itself in smoke and the thud of automatic rifle fire and the shouts of protest as the schoolchildren of Soweto rebelled against the education system. It gave new meaning to the question I had only heard formulated as an academic proposition: how long will South Africa survive?

In those words resided the fear of white South Africa. Those who uttered them were asking how long apartheid could be maintained, or how many more years there were before the chaos of Africa brought potholes to the highways, power failures, food shortages, the collapse of hospitals, the breakdown of the telephone system, the end of education, blood in the streets. Prior to 1976 it was a divisive question because it sought to explain the country in terms of settlers and natives. It invented both groups and it gave to the former all the positive attributes of civilization and to the latter all the dark, brutal qualities of savage and primitive peoples. It was the sort of question that had to be asked in order to keep the distinctions clear and in order to keep reinforcing the narrative white South Africa wished to live. What was out there was 'incomprehensible frenzy', 'a swirl of black limbs, a mass of hands clapping, of feet stamping, of bodies swaying, of eyes rolling', a 'wild and passionate uproar' as Conrad described it in *Heart of Darkness*. I think that after 1976 this narrative of separateness was shattered: it was suddenly very clear that the other world was not another world at all, but a part of where we lived.

I first asked the question of how long South Africa would survive in 1974. That I asked it so late in my life says much about the comfortable country in which I grew up. As I have said, it was a place separated by apartheid from all other places. It was a country that existed only in our minds and we maintained its privileges by never venturing, either in thought or deed, beyond its walls. When we let in those from outside they came only to clean our houses or mow our lawns. But even then we did not see them, and at night they returned to the darkness beyond the gates. This was the sort of fiction and metaphor that apartheid created and we lived out. It seems strange to write now about this colony I have not lived in for a long time. It is like describing a foreign country where I sojourned briefly, uneasily.

In 1974 there were some unmistakable signs that the story I had been told of how my life would be conducted was a lie. Revolutions in Mozambique and Angola ended Portuguese colonialism in Africa. And so asking how much time South Africa had left was tantamount to questioning all the premises on which I had based my expectations. But the cracks in the story were not immediately obvious. The first time I asked the question I was given the simple answer of twenty to twenty-five years. The person who made the assessment was a political reporter. I was twenty-three. His conclusion amounted to a lifetime.

Three years later I read R. W. Johnson's *How Long Will South Africa Survive?*. He wrote:

> . . . pondering the future of South Africa's White Establishment is no easy task. It would seem a historical certainty that it must eventually pass away or fall. Yet to ask 'how long will (white) South Africa survive?' is, in Herman Kahn's famous phrase, to 'think about the unthinkable.' So many factors are relevant. Most are complex, many are humanly repugnant and some not a little frightening. One has to think about them all the same.

Johnson was writing after the historic events of June 1976. The question was no longer academic; everywhere I saw and heard the images from Yeats's poem 'The Second Coming'. The falcon was away, the gyres were widening, a blood-dimmed tide had been loosed, the ceremony of innocence was drowned. Surely Yeats's 'rough beast' was history, and surely its hour had come round at last.

In June 1976 I was serving my notice month with a conservative news magazine called *To the Point*. I had decided to leave partly because I needed a change and partly because my copy was now subject to the editor's approval and I found the patriarchal eye stifling. I had gone from being the carefree movie and book reviewer to a reporter who had to be watched in case any of his naïve attacks on censorship slipped through. Not only had I deigned to criticize the Minister of Information, Connie Mulder, but I had tried to publish a review of Martin Amis's novel *Dead Babies*, praising its moral tone. Unbeknown to me the editor's secretary was simultaneously making representations to the censorship board to have the novel banned. By chance she had seen the book on my desk, read a few pages, and recognized that here was an evil thing indeed. (Like Salman Rushdie's *The Satanic Verses, Dead Babies* remains banned to this day.)

So during June 1976 I was winding down my job. I spent the afternoon of Wednesday 16th in a cinema watching Antonioni's *The Passenger*. When I came out Johannesburg's evening newspaper, *The Star*, showed Soweto in flames.

The next day I persuaded the magazine's news editor to let me go to Soweto. He was not convinced he needed a witness there. He maintained that a 'wrap-up' could be written from the newspapers and the wire-service reports. I persisted and he went to talk to the editor. He returned even more sceptical but said if I wished to go I would have to take my own car and that the magazine could not cover it for damage. But I was not to worry as the insurers would pay out for my death or injury. Like so many news editors he had a strange sense of humour.

Visiting Soweto was not easy on Thursday 17th. The police had roadblocks at all the main routes into the township and were letting only residents through. I was clearly not a resident. I spent the afternoon at a roadblock not far from the Baragwanath Hospital, talking to jittery travelling salesmen, medical representatives and doctors who had driven through a barrage of stones and rocks as they left the hospital. Most of them were cut and bleeding. Some were also crying. Their cars had few unshattered windows. I made notes and took photographs. One of the photographs was of a police troop carrier as it went through the roadblock and on towards the smoke and mayhem that I could only imagine would be revealed round the corner. A police officer approached me. He told me I was not to photograph the police. He demanded the camera and opened it and pulled out the film and left it lying black and shiny like a sloughed snakeskin upon the ground. I went home. And as I drove over the ridge into Johannesburg's northern suburbs I wondered that the fear and the excitement and the sense of possibility could be so completely contained behind a roadblock. Here it was an ordinary winter's evening: brown lawns, leafless streets, commuters driving home, house lights going on, the sun flattening into the haze on the horizon.

On the Friday morning I went to Alexandra, a township not far from the magazine's office. It was not visible from the fifteenth-floor windows, but the black towers of smoke that hung over it were. I parked the car on Louis Botha Avenue and walked to the township. It was on fire. All I could think of were the opening lines of Mongane Wally Serote's poem to the place of his birth:

Were it possible to say,
Mother, I have seen more beautiful mothers,
A most loving mother,
And tell her there I will go,
Alexandra, I would have long gone from you.

I walked to where a small shopping centre was being looted and burned. Something was happening that did not have to do with looting and burning. Certainly there was glass everywhere. There were large rocks on the road. People shouted and screamed. Down the street a Putco bus burned, sending up a vast dark cloud. Police with pump-action shotguns fired at figures in the smog below. And there was a sense of something stirring. This, I suddenly realized, was history. History was not only the past. It was not only dates and places and events. History was also now. It was the smell of burning rubber. It was the crack of the guns. But mostly it was the shouting: the fear and the jubilation. The chaos. A police Hippo drew up and the policemen who had been shooting piled in and this Wellsian vehicle disappeared into the smoke. It was a bit like a dream. Figures came and went. Events seemed un-connected, spontaneous and violent. Someone was tugging at my arm. 'Run!' he shouted. 'For God's sake, run!' He pulled me and I staggered after him. There was a Valiant sedan ahead of us, moving slowly, its back doors open. Anxious faces urged us on. I was thrust in. The car acceler-ated off. 'We have lost everything,' said the man next to me, the man who had dragged me away. 'Everything.' The others in the car said nothing. They dropped me on Louis Botha Avenue. I went back to the magazine to write about what I had seen.

There are two footnotes to this story:

That week's issue of the magazine carried my short eye-witness account at the bottom of one of the news pages. The cover story was on South Africa's mineral potential. The editor, John Poorter, had weekly meetings with Prime Minister B. J. Vorster, who may have influenced his decision to down-play the riots, if not directly then at least as a form of self-censorship.

Now, eighteen years later, I could not remember whether the police troop carriers of those days were known as Hippos or Casspirs. I telephoned the police museum, coincidentally located in Muizenberg.

'No, no, no,' said the helpful sergeant who answered the phone. 'The Casspir saw very good service in the township riots during the Eighties but in 'seventy-six the police used Hippos. But don't let me tell you about it, there's a captain standing here who was part of those riots.'

The captain took the phone.

'What's your name?' he demanded.

I told him.

'What do you want the information for?'

I told him. There was something perversely comforting about his aggressiveness. He was talking the way I expected policemen to talk. Or, rather, not talking but interrogating. He wanted to ask the questions.

I asked him what vehicles the police used in Alexandra in June 1976.

'Jeeps and patrol cars,' he replied.

'Only jeeps and patrol cars?'

'Ja, mostly.'

'But what about troop carriers?'

'Ja, we had troop carriers.'

'The Hippo?'

'Ja, but not in all the townships.'

'But you did use the Hippo in Alex?'

'Yes.'

Such a simple detail, a historical detail of no danger to the state, and yet he could not but be evasive. He could not shake off the way he had been for all those years. He could not adapt like the young sergeant, who apparently believed the police had as much claim to the events of June '76 as the Soweto youths. The pervading spirit of reconciliation could manifest itself in some absurd and bizarre ways.

The events of June 1976 seem, more than any of the other defiance campaigns, to have set in motion all that was to follow. At the time the prison authorities on Robben Island viewed them so seriously that for two months they managed to suppress news of the riots from leaking through to the prisoners. But once new political prisoners began to arrive on the Island, reports of the insurrection reached Mandela and those incarcerated with him. The stories engendered such hopes in the political prisoners that some believed the National Party government was about to be overthrown. There was talk that it would be a matter of weeks, months at the most, before they were released.

Mandela, Walter Sisulu, Govan Mbeki and the other 'Treason Trialists' had already spent thirteen years there. It was to be another thirteen years before they would be freed. And even then Mandela was not prepared to accept freedom until it was quite clear that the National Party intended moving towards a democratic constitution.

But on Sunday 11 February 1990 the day came, as it had to, when the man who had been found guilty of treason and sentenced to life imprisonment walked out of jail.

Jill and I, and thousands upon thousands of others, went to Cape Town's Grand Parade to hear his first public speech in twenty-seven years. It was one of those moments in history when the past was reclaimed. That it should have been at Cape Town, not far from where d'Almeida was killed by the Khoikhoi five centuries earlier, was appropriate. That it should have been on the Grand Parade, where in the first centuries of white rule the colonial armies had paraded, was also fitting. That it should be at a place where for half a century Cape Town had celebrated Queen Victoria's birthday seemed justly ironic. I wondered if the ghost of King Cetshwayo, brought up from his dungeon at the nearby castle in 1882 to watch the Queen's soldiers honour her on the Parade, had returned to smile in triumph.

The day was hot and our armpits were clammy and the sweat beaded constantly along our upper lips: a relentless Cape Town day in February with one hundred per cent humidity and the sun pounding on the granite face of the mountain and pulsing out of the sky in white bolts. Yet a phalanx of people *toyi-toyi*ed round and round the Grand Parade singing songs of triumph and freedom. They were soaked with perspiration yet they kept on, never wavering for a moment in their energy or their intention. Each time they passed us some leered into our faces with raised fists; some, laughing, tried to draw us into their ranks, which were swelling as people began to gather on the square.

For the midday hours we found a thin shade beneath some ornamental trees. We sat on the gravel, huddled in the shadow: Jill and I, an old man and his young grand-daughter. He had some peaches which he cut into segments and shared among us. It was the only refreshment we had had in hours and I bit quickly into the fruit, eager to have the juice run sweet and sharp into the well of my mouth. The man raised his hand and pointed with his knife towards the phalanx.

'What do you think of them?' he asked.

It was a rhetorical question and I made no attempt to answer it.

'Look at them,' he said. 'Savages!'

He chewed on his peach.

'You know, my family also suffered under apartheid. We had to leave our house so that whites could live in it. We had to sit at the back of trains and at the back of buses. We couldn't go to the bioscopes or the theatres or the beaches, but still we've managed. My father started a new shop. We have a house. We have cars. We make a good living. But look at this. We are not part of this. How can these people run a country?'

I must admit I looked at the sweating, yelling horde and knew I was not part of it either. But did that matter? It certainly did not matter to them. And I did not really think it mattered to me. So I shrugged in answer to his questions and he shook his head in sadness. But perhaps also in fear.

When we had finished the peaches his granddaughter started tugging at his trousers, whining that she wanted to go home.

'But it's still two hours to wait,' he said to her.

She persisted.

'OK, OK,' he sighed. And turned to us and first shook Jill's hand and then mine.

'I hope it will be all right,' he said, but I did not know whether he was referring to the crowd or the future. They moved off, his granddaughter leading him through the thickening crush. I watched them go, wondering at the emotions that had drawn him here to witness the first free hours of the world's most famous political prisoner. Surely he had come out of some sense of celebration, or maybe to pay respects, to show that all those locked years of one man's life had not been wasted? When he woke up this morning what was it that brought him here? He was gone and I would never know. But I did know that he had seen the future and he was unhappy. The present may deny him, yet he had learned to live within it. What was to come filled him with dread.

Soon the press of people forced us to stand. The *toyi-toyi*ers had stopped because the crowd now filled the Parade. People had climbed the statues; others had even found footholds halfway up the streetlight poles. On the balcony of the city hall Allan Boesak tried to keep the crowd calm.

'Please keep still, please keep patient,' he pleaded as a ripple passed through the throng and those in front were pushed against the stone walls. 'He'll soon be here. He has left the prison. You do not have long to wait.'

A vendor came round selling soft drinks. We bought a can of Coke which was warm and sweet but at least it was liquid. A teenager watched us drinking. We tried to avoid his eyes but he started towards us nevertheless.

'Give us a drink,' he said, and snatched the can from Jill's hand. He finished the contents and threw the tin at our feet. '*Amandla!*' he shouted, laughing as we cringed away from his aggression. Then, unable to resist it, he screamed '*Amandla*' again before turning into the crowd.

We shuddered, unnerved by this blatant hostility.

A police helicopter came over the towerblocks and circled the Parade, the noise alarming and irritating and raising anger in the crowd. I noticed there were policemen with rifles on the roof of the parking-garage behind us and also on the post office building to our right. I pointed them out to Jill. Should we go, I was about to ask, but she read my thoughts: 'No. Not after all this time.'

Some friends shouldering their way out of the crowd joined us. You shouldn't stand here, they cajoled. If there's trouble you'll be trapped.

They moved on but we stayed where we were until the shooting started.

By half-past four Mandela had still not arrived. Despite the wait and the heat the crowd remained good-natured except that on the fringes things were beginning to fray and break up. Some teenage boys, clutching running shoes and T-shirts, dashed past. Then there was a shout and a surge of people rolled towards us. I grabbed Jill and we sheltered behind a telephone booth. People rushed by laughing, waving the jackets and shirts and shoes they had looted. Monitors tried to calm the situation, tried to prevent the looting. I heard the hollow detonations of rifles being fired. It came from behind us. We ran. Hand in hand, ducking behind cars, we ran. Stretching across an intersection was a line of policemen, blue, armed, their Alsatians, fanged and barking, leaping against the leashes. The street was littered with tins and stones. Two men stood in the middle taunting the police. The one held a rock in his hand, the other a cold-drink tin. We swerved away and went down a side street and through the lane where the flower sellers usually sat into Adderley Street and across it and into empty streets where it was just an ordinary Sunday.

When we got home there was a message on the answering-machine from two British photographers asking if we could put them up for the night. An hour later they arrived.

What happened, we wanted to know? Had there been more shooting? What time did Mandela get there?

Yeah, they said. There'd been more shooting. They'd got pictures of bodies on the tar.

Then they turned the house into a news agency and commandeered the telephone.

Later, when they had gone out to supper, I telephoned the news desk of the *Cape Times* because there was no news of the event on the radio. I was told Mandela had arrived about seven-thirty, had said his piece, which had been uninspiring party rhetoric, and was gone. I was told one person had died: a teenager who was shot while he snatched bottles from a liquor store's broken window.

It was to be four years before Nelson Mandela would again address the crowds massed on the Grand Parade from the balcony of the City Hall. This time, though, he would be President. This time he would have been driven there from Parliament, not from a prison.

That morning of Monday 9 May 1994, the new Members of Parliament took their oaths in the building that had been the centre of white domination since the previous century.

As he walked up the steps Tokyo Sexwale, newly elected premier of the Johannesburg region, said, 'I never thought it would come to this. We were committed to the violent overthrow of the National Party government, to the removal of the regime by force.' He smiled and waved at the photographers. 'I feel victorious,' he said.

Inside, the new democrats raised their hands and committed themselves to the country and the constitution. When nominations were called for the position of president there was only one.

Chief Justice Michael Corbett announced: 'I accordingly declare Mr Nelson Rolihlahla Mandela duly elected as the President of the Republic of South Africa.' MPs and visitors in the public gallery stood up and applauded and cheered and ululated and cried. Mandela, with a white rose in his lapel, looked on. And the Island within him kept him serious and dignified.

On the floor the official praise singer to the president launched into a tribute that regaled too the ancestors and the martyrs and the heroes. He said that the blood of the black people was thundering, the mountain was tumbling, and the bones of those such as Chris Hani, Oliver Tambo and Albert Luthuli had risen in pride to celebrate their people's freedom.

And then Mandela was taken down to the Grand Parade where again the crowd roared for him.

Beside him Archbishop Tutu, resplendent in purple vestments, gave his blessing to the people. He said this day had been waiting for three hundred years, 'this day of liberation for all of us, black and white together'. He told the crowd they were the 'rainbow people' and exhorted them to welcome our 'brand-new out-of-the-box state president'.

Who raised his hands in greeting and said, 'Today we celebrate not a victory for a party but a victory for all the people of South Africa. We come not as conquerors but as fellow-citizens.'

I listened to this on the radio. I listened as Mandela summoned from his life the Island which brought with it the shades of other men who had been imprisoned there. I thought of the more famous among them. Of Siyolo, hated by the colonial militias during the Eighth Frontier War of 1850–53, who was first sentenced to death and then banished to the Island. And of Maqoma, who had also caused devastation among the British forces during the frontier wars.

In the South African Library there is a glass-plate photograph of Maqoma, probably taken during his imprisonment on the Island. It shows a strong face beneath the bald dome of his forehead. The line of the lips is chiselled, the eyes are unwavering. The library has another photograph, taken in 1859, of the chiefs exiled to the Island from their lands to the east of what the Cape Colony had declared its border. They are standing before a large hut. Some people, including the wives of Siyolo and Maqoma, huddle in blankets on the ground. The scrub is sparse and low; the sand shows through the vegetation. It is a bleak image, utterly bleak.

This is part of what Mandela takes with him. It is what I mean by saying he personifies our history. And it is why he carries a symbolic value that is greater than Mandela the man. This is not an easy burden and it places a responsibility on him that is unfair. But then, like writers, we do not treat our characters fairly. We are inclined to make these demands of people, and we are inclined to measure them against the moment. In a way, F. W. de Klerk was also measured.

When the crowd sang 'Nkosi Sikelel' iAfrika' on that sunny Monday afternoon, de Klerk too was standing on the City Hall balcony, but to the back and to the side, in the shadow. He had been dutifully cheered by some of the people gathered there, but his name had also brought a rumble of discontent across the Parade. However, it should be recorded that he, as probably no one had done before, knowingly gave up power. From the moment he took office in 1989 it was clear that this was his intention and it is remarkable that he never altered in this course. These things should be remembered about F. W. de Klerk. Just as it should be realized that if his predecessor, P. W. Botha, had not had a minor stroke, South Africa might well have been the same country today that it was in 1988.

That Mandela and de Klerk have stood up to the moment is, to say the least, fortuitous. It is said that in the lives of most nations an outstanding figure will arise only once a century. To have two, and to have them both alive at the same time, is extraordinary. At the moment, in these winter days, we have this to be thankful for.

*

Two weeks after the inauguration, Mandela gave his State of the Nation speech in Parliament. It was remarkable for a number of reasons. It addressed the needs of the present but it placed them within the context of the past. More importantly, it raised the ghost of an Afrikaans poet who in July 1965 at the age of thirty-one walked into the cold Atlantic waters off Mouille Point in Cape Town and drowned herself. She drowned herself because she could not abide the injustices of apartheid. Her name was Ingrid Jonker. Mandela referred only to her in his speech but her name is linked indelibly with another. In the same month and halfway across the world, the writer Nat Nakasa, exiled from his country, jumped to his death from a New York towerblock. It is well to remember this. And in a country where poetry has little value it is well to set down some words of William Plomer's elegy to this woman and this man:

> Where a dry tide of sheep
> Ebbs between rocks
> In a miasma of dust.
> Where time is wool;
> He is not there.
>
> Where towers of green water
> Crash, re-shaping
> White contours of sand,
> Velvet to a bare foot;
> She is not there.

These are the opening stanzas of Plomer's 'The Taste of the Fruit'.

What Mandela did with his reference to Jonker was subtle and deeply compassionate. He made her live again and, by reading one of her poems, acknowledged a sense of humanity which is often absent from our society. In a land where the social contract has been so disdained and, in places, continues to be vilified, Mandela's words provided some kind of measure:

'The time will come when our nation will honour the memory of all the sons, the daughters, the mothers, the fathers, the youth and the children who, by their thoughts and deeds, gave us the right to assert with pride that we are South Africans, that we are Africans and that we are citizens of the world.

'The certainties that come with age tell me that among these we shall find an Afrikaner woman who transcended a particular experience and became a South African, an African and a citizen of the world.

'Her name is Ingrid Jonker.

'She was both a poet and a South African. She was both an Afrikaner and African. She was both an artist and a human being.

'In the midst of despair, she celebrated hope. Confronted by death, she asserted the beauty of life.

'In the dark days when all seemed hopeless in our country, when many refused to hear her resonant voice, she took her own life.

'To her and others like her, we owe a debt to life itself.

'To her and others like her, we owe a commitment to the poor, the oppressed, the wretched and the despised.

'In the aftermath of the massacre at the anti-pass demonstration in Sharpeville she wrote that:

'"The child is not dead
    the child lifts his fists against his mother
        who shouts Afrika! . . .

The child is not dead
Not at Langa nor at Nyanga

86

nor at Orlando nor at Sharpeville
nor at the police post at Philippi
where he lies with a bullet through his brain . . .

the child is present at all assemblies and law-giving
the child peers through the windows of houses
and into the hearts of mothers
this child who only wanted to play in the sun at
   Nyanga
is everywhere

the child grown to a man treks on through all Afrika
the child grown to a giant journeys
over the whole world

without a pass!"

'And in this glorious vision, she instructs that our endeavours must be about the liberation of the woman, the emancipation of the man and the liberty of the child.

'It is these things that we must achieve to give meaning to our presence in this chamber and to give purpose to our occupancy of the seat of government.

'And so we must, constrained by and yet regardless of the accumulated effect of our historical burdens, seize the time to define for ourselves what we want to make of our shared destiny.'

Towards the end of the address he referred again to Jonker:

'Tomorrow, on Africa Day, the dream of Ingrid Jonker will come to fruition. The child grown to a man will trek through all Afrika. The child grown to a giant will journey over the whole world – without a pass!'

As I listened to Mandela's speeches over those days I realized I was listening to something new. Gone were the quick slogans and the cheap rhetoric that had aroused his followers during the election roadshows and before that during the defiance campaigns. Nor was the dogmatism that had immobilized the words of the previous governments anywhere in evidence. Instead, despite a few glib phrases, there was an obvious straining for fine language. In the sentences a new rhythm was manifest, and an awareness of words and how they linked to one another and how they stirred in the imaginations of those who heard them. Care was being given to this language. It was being treated as fragile and in need of rejuvenation. There may have been no memorable phrases but there was an appreciation of language that had probably not been heard in political speeches since the defiance rallies of the Fifties. I felt that in a way Mandela was asking people to reimagine themselves. Perhaps he saw the election days as the beginning of this process and was hoping for a greater change.

5

To many people the election was a miracle. This was the word they repeatedly used when discussing those days. It occurred on radio talk shows; it occurred in panel discussions on television. It was used almost in the sense that there had been divine intervention. As I listened to these commentators I saw God going out into the karoo to speak with the Maleficents. I saw Him standing on the black rocks as they gathered about and I heard their spokesman shout: 'How long dost thou not judge and avenge our blood?' And I saw God raise His arms to pacify them.

I suppose it was understandable, this longing for the miraculous that would show we had not been left to our history. How apt then that at the presidential inauguration Rabbi Harris should quote these verses from Isaiah: 'For a small moment have I forsaken thee; but with great mercies will I gather thee.'

And: 'In a little wrath I hid my face from thee for a moment . . .'

And: 'Violence shall no more be heard in thy land . . .'

They were ringing words, deeply intoned. They seemed to have been written for this moment.

Even the President started talking about a 'new spirit abroad in the land'. It was enough to pack me with emotion

and to make me shiver. It was then I recalled a passage in
J. M. Coetzee's *Age of Iron* and went cold:

> Let me tell you, when I walk upon this land, this South
> Africa, I have a gathering feeling of walking upon black
> faces. They are dead but their spirit has not left them. They
> lie there heavy and obdurate, waiting for my feet to pass,
> waiting for me to go, waiting to be raised up again.
> Millions of figures of pig-iron floating under the skin of the
> earth. The age of iron waiting to return.

In a land where the context was violence, where most of
the stories that were told made up a narrative of violence,
how else could such moments of good will be seen, if not
as miracles? How else, indeed? And when a large part of
the population had got down on its Christian knees and
prayed for peace, was this not an answer to the prayers?
Was this astonishing event not a miracle?

And had we not entered now a time of grace?

The tyrants and the terrorists had sat down together in
Parliament. Afrikaner patriots had hailed the new democratic South Africa as an event of liberation for themselves.
And in return the new president had talked about 'a
generosity of spirit . . . so abundantly displayed by the
oppressed and suffering people who have mandated their
leaders and representatives to politically negotiate a future
of peace, forgiveness and inclusivity'.

On television Adelaide Tambo, widow of former ANC
President Oliver Tambo, said, 'I must thank white South
Africans, because since the elections were announced they
have been very supportive. The mood of the country is so
beautiful.'

South Africa was back in the Commonwealth, and once
more part of the United Nations. Mandela had opened the
annual meeting of the Organization of African Unity. He

had spoken of South Africa being the breadbasket of the southern continent. Yesterday's newspaper had announced an airlift of medical supplies and food to the refugees of Rwanda's civil war. Pepsi Cola had returned. Other major companies, it was said, were about to invest hundreds of millions of dollars.

'Do you know what this could mean?' said my father as we talked about these miraculous days. 'Could you imagine how this country might flourish?' There was so much hope in his voice.

But was it a miracle? Or was it an expression of one of those good moments that sometimes happen in history? That have happened in all histories. Fancifully, we believe such events happened more frequently in South Africa than elsewhere; these strange moments that are strange because of their goodness. Strange because mostly our context is not good. Mostly it is wretched.

And yet it has been common throughout these last years to hear politicians, businesspeople, Black Sash presidents, priests, the banned, the tortured, the survivors of those murdered by the state or by the armies of the right and the left, speak of a 'reservoir of good will'. In this country where water is scarce and so much of the land is semi-desert we choose to use a word like 'reservoir'. A word that tells of something set aside, something reserved, something stored. And of self-restraint. A word that conjures up images of muddy pans in the late light of the Free State, or the deep green of Clanwilliam Dam against the granite of the Cedarberg Mountains, or the coolness of the water in a farm's corrugated-iron storage tank next to a windmill where beetles swim through the clarity. These reservoirs are always quiet places. Sometimes they are stroked by wind. More often they give back the exactness of their surroundings.

In Parliament a member commenting on the election spoke of how 'people decided to do good'. Without doubt this society which all political analysis describes as 'divided' went out and did good. Did it in the name of liberation but also because there was a negotiated settlement, an interim constitution, and a man who spoke to it through the power of his personality. Doing good was something of which even this tortured society was capable. And not against the odds but because of them. If we did not live so constantly in the clamour of evil, would we have been able to see so clearly? I do not think so.

'What is so amazing about this country', the Nigerian writer Kole Omotosa told me one evening at a cocktail party to launch a new publishing venture designed to promote black literature and literacy and backed solidly by one of the bulwarks of Afrikaner publishing, 'is that once the ANC were in the transitional government they dropped the vocabulary of the struggle. No other African states have done that. They have all carried the ideology into the years of government. Not a week after he was in power I heard Terror Lekota [premier of the Free State] telling people to go back to work, that the days of marches were over. The thing is these people don't think like Africans. Their attitudes are very Western, not at all the way they are in other parts of Africa. They have assimilated Western attitudes to a far greater degree than elsewhere.'

Perhaps it was because of the constitution, because of Mandela, because of the 'reservoir of good will', that things happened the way they did. It was a high point in our history and probably nothing like it will occur again. But I think it was enough that it happened once, that at least there was this story that could be told in any future turned suddenly dark.

*

But it is a very fragile story and this should never be forgotten. And if it is to be seen in its delicateness and if it is to be given the right emphasis it has to be seen against what has gone before.

On the morning after the presidential inauguration I read a piece by R. W. Johnson in the *London Review of Books*. I was still gripped by the euphoria of the previous day and what he wrote seemed so wrong, at least in its tone. It showed a country in chaos. One sentence I read over and over again: 'Everything's a mess, nothing's anything like ready, there's bound to be much more killing.' Johnson had been writing before the election and the paper was dated 28 April. I did not know how to respond to this. It was all true and yet it was not. It left out what I had seen in people and heard on the radio. It did not allow for a moment of triumph, no matter how vulnerable that moment might be. Nor did it give a hint that this might have been possible. Towards the end of the article he said we were about to start history anew. But, of course, we could not start history again: we were part of it and lived in it, and we had to deal with it every day of our lives. In the weeks to come there would be much talk about 'new beginnings', about 'wiping the slate clean', about 'making a break with the past'. People said this with the best of intentions but they were all wrong and paradoxically it was Johnson's article that showed me why. He gave a telling summary of what we had recently lived through and made me go back to a file I kept which was labelled simply VIOLENCE. This, in part, was what Johnson wrote:

> It's hard to know what would count as normality in a society where scores of Africans can be shot down in the street by other Africans and no one even dreams of apprehending their killers. Where Eugene Terre'Blanche

can appear on TV and boast that the AWB's raid into Bophuthatswana was a 'victory' because his men killed a hundred innocent Africans, and no one even suggests that in that case he should be arrested for murder. Where taxi-wars rage, leaving scores dead. Where men with Kalash-nikovs board commuter trains shouting 'Bulala aba thakathi' (Kill the witches) and then proceed to hurl any 'witches' they find off the moving train. Where a disturbed woman with a criminal record can be elected head of her party's women's section, an MP, and . . . to the Cabinet. Where Afrikaner conservatives insist, under threat of war, on a *volkstaat* but cannot for the life of them tell you where they want it to be.

This describes us, it provides the context of our lives. It has always to be remembered. It can never be forgotten. It made me look through my file.

I found that, on the day in October 1993 when it was announced that F. W. de Klerk and Nelson Mandela had been awarded the Nobel Peace Prize, the murderers of the much respected ANC veteran Chris Hani were sentenced to death by hanging. Across the street from the Rand Supreme Court where this verdict was being handed down, mourners were gathering in the Johannesburg Central Methodist Church. They were there to attend a memorial service for five young people killed the previous Friday when South African Defence Force soldiers attacked what they believed was a PAC stronghold in Umtata. In the twenty-seven-minute assault they raked the building with gun-fire. Some of the victims had as many as eighteen bullet wounds. Two of the dead were under twelve years old. The raid was said to have been authorized by de Klerk. During the service the mourners started chanting: 'In the name of Jesus Christ . . . one settler, one bullet.' Three days later Mandela was interviewed on Radio

Metro. He condemned de Klerk for the raid and said of the Hani murderers that although the ANC was against capital punishment it would be persuaded by the will of the people in this instance.

That day of the Nobel Peace announcement the *Weekly Mail & Guardian* reported that between July and September eighty-five commuters had been murdered on trains in the Witwatersrand and 105 people had been injured. The next day the *Cape Times* had stories about four people who had been killed in fighting in Natal; a sixty-five-year-old man who had been stabbed to death at Nyanga; two policemen who had been shot to death on the East Rand; a schoolgirl who had saved the life of a woman being stabbed by three attackers. A week later *Vrye Weekblad* declared South Africa one of the bloodiest places in the world. That Friday Michael Phama was convicted in the Rand Supreme Court of shooting dead twenty-one people. Of those, sixteen had been Inkatha supporters on a peace march. During the trial the judge called society 'brutal', 'disturbed', 'dislocated'. During the trial emotions ran so high that new violence was perpetrated in the East Rand townships. More people died. The ANC never criticized Phama. One senior spokesman told a reporter that Phama was a kind of hero. 'Actually, I quite liked the man,' he said.

It would be daunting to catalogue every act of murder and assault that marked the days of January, February, March and April 1994. I could not stand to read such a litany of death. I would despair. Anyone reading it would despair. It would condemn this society. We would be seen as brutal, disturbed and dislocated. But I have to give some idea of what that time was like.

I remember bomb blasts and the obituary notices of those slain. I remember hearing a man crying on the radio after the bodies of his employees had been found in the dongas and grass of kwaZulu. They had gone to distribute voter education pamphlets. They were tortured and mutilated in a school classroom by men wielding pangas and knobkerries. Then they were taken out into the veld and shot. Seven of them. The man cried and it was the first time that I had heard such publicly expressed incomprehensible, bewildered grief. Why? he kept asking. Why? Why? Why?

I remember the photograph of three AWB men in their khaki shorts and shirts lying dead next to their old Mercedes. I remember the photograph of a black soldier shooting them. In a recent novel I had described the gratuitous murder of a black diamond miner chanced upon on the veld by a group of mostly white bandits. It had provoked a similar image: the gun as an extension of the arm, pointing, sentencing, executing. This newspaper photograph was the mirror image. It signalled the end of the frontier mentality. The end of colonialism. The end of apartheid.

Before they died the men had been part of an AWB convoy of vehicles which had driven through the centre of Mmabatho shooting at people in the streets. The AWB was in Mmabatho to help President Lucas Mangope of Bophuthatswana, who was being ousted by his people because he did not want them to vote in the April elections. President Lucas Mangope was an apartheid dictator and his people had had enough. They went on to the streets to get rid of him. It was into this maelstrom that the AWB commandos rode in their Mercedes and *bakkie*-vans and Mazdas. And they were shot at by paratroopers and the convoy was scattered and now the old Mercedes came to a stop among an angry crowd.

The driver lay bleeding to death on the dirt road. A big white man with a bushy beard crouched by the open front door, his hands raised in surrender. A third man cowered

96

in the rear seat, then slid out and lay against the back wheel.

'Black bastards,' he muttered in Afrikaans, and the crowd shouted at him: 'Who asked you to come here? Are you sorry now?'

The big bearded man was forced to lie on his belly while soldiers frisked him for weapons. He tried to tell them his companion was not dead. But no one was listening to him.

'Fuck it,' he screamed, 'somebody just get a fucking ambulance. Please God help us, get us some medical help.'

Then a soldier with an R4 rifle shot him and shot the man braced against the back wheel and fired some more rounds into their lifeless bodies.

There was a photograph taken some minutes after this which I could not get out of my mind either. It showed the Mercedes and on the road behind it military vehicles approaching. The three AWB men lay sprawled on the dirt. A metre from them crouched some photographers behind their cameras and lenses. They looked like heavily beaked vultures hopping forward to rend the kill.

I remember a photograph of Zulu warriors gathered to hear King Goodwill Zwelithini. So many of them were armed with AK47s.

In my file was a clipping of a piece written by Ken Owen, editor of the *Sunday Times*. He said, 'With only five weeks to go nerves are fraying, tempers shortening. The country is awash with rumours and alarums.' He ended: 'The centre is holding, but barely. We must go through with elections so that we can return to order . . . and establish a true democracy.'

The same issue of his newspaper carried a map of the most violent areas in kwaZulu/Natal. It showed a coastal band about one hundred kilometres wide from the south-ern border with Transkei to the northern border with

Mozambique. The caption read: 'Since 1985 some 12,000 have died in the Natal wars.'

In my diary on 30 March I made a note of a telephone conversation I had had with my mother. I don't know why I wrote it down except that sometimes the old habit of making notes while I talk on the telephone still asserts itself. She asked how to make melba toast. I described to her the technique of freezing a loaf of white bread and then cutting the thin slices while the bread was frozen. She said she was going to make melba toast just in case there were any food shortages. At the time rumours of possible shortages were denuding supermarket shelves of candles and tinned foods and dry goods and gas. My mother said, 'They say people should stock up with essentials because there is going to be trouble.' The trouble would be electricity cuts due to sabotage and a complete disruption of the food supply. I wanted to know where the story had come from. She said a policeman had told someone who had told a friend who had told her. I said that she should not take the rumours too seriously. But then stocking up with melba toast did not seem to indicate a firm commitment to impending disaster.

In the beginning of April a state of emergency was declared in kwaZulu/Natal. A few days later an Inkatha march through the centre of Johannesburg ended with fifty-three people dead and hundreds wounded. Many people had been shot by snipers firing from the roofs. Buthelezi declared 27 and 28 April days of mourning. There was every indication that with Inkatha boycotting the elections things would go horribly awry in kwaZulu/Natal and on the East Rand where heavy fighting was a daily condition.

And then, for the believers in miracles, a miracle oc-curred. An aeroplane developed engine trouble and had to go back to an airport where a man was waiting to convince Mangosuthu Buthelezi that if he did not take part in the election his political career would be finished and his name would not be found in the history to come.

How much of this story is to be believed I do not know. But in days of heightened emotion a coincidence can take on a weight and meaning it might not normally be accorded, and for that reason it becomes part of the mythology of the time. Besides, I like the idea that history can be determined by the poor performance of an aeroplane engine.

A few days prior to this event, Dr Henry Kissinger and Lord Carrington had come to South Africa to try and solve the 'Buthelezi problem' and bring him into the elections. Unbeknown to everyone at the time, and completely overshadowed by the imminence of the two international mediators, so had a Kenyan academic named Washington 'Sipwap' Okumu. We learned later that he was a long-standing friend of Buthelezi's, but he received no media attention until after the announcement that Inkatha had agreed to take part in the elections. And then he had his fifteen minutes of fame and disappeared again. Now it is difficult believing he really existed.

Kissinger and Carrington never got a chance to sit down with Buthelezi. At the last minute the chief found the preconditions to the talks unsatisfactory and withdrew. After that all attempts at compromise failed and Kissinger and Carrington were forced to leave. Clearly they were just wasting their time. On the afternoon of their departure from Johannesburg, Okumu also said goodbye to Buthelezi. They shook hands in the foyer of the Carlton Hotel.

'Where do we go to from here?' asked the troubled Inkatha leader.

'Look, my brother,' said Okumu, 'I will stay overnight. Tomorrow we can talk about what you can do.'

But the next morning Buthelezi left for Lanseria Airport before Okumu could contact him. Okumu phoned the airport and Buthelezi agreed to wait but he said that he had a meeting with the Zulu King in kwaZulu and could not spare much time.

So he waited and after half an hour, when Okumu had not arrived, he decided he could wait no longer. His plane took off.

From the terminal building Okumu watched it disappear towards the south. He felt defeated by the pressure of time. He had a bad taste in his mouth. For some minutes he felt lost and very alone. Then he went outside to the waiting taxi to return to Johannesburg and book a flight to Nairobi. But before he reached the car he received a message that he was to stay, that the plane was coming back.

'They've got engine problems,' he was told; 'they will be back in a few minutes.'

Which was how Okumu got to speak to Buthelezi. What he told Buthelezi was this: 'My brother, I am going to speak from the heart as a friend and Christian believer about the serious consequences which will accrue if you do not take part in this election. You will lose your position after April 27, you will lose your power base and your only option will be guerrilla warfare. You must drop your demands.'

And Buthelezi replied, 'My brother, it is too late for me to participate in the election. And I cannot go into the election unless the position of the King is secured. It would look as if I am just looking after my own interests. But Nelson Mandela trusts you. Why don't you negotiate between Mr Mandela and President de Klerk and see what you can arrange?'

Which is how the Inkatha Freedom Party entered the elections. And a day before the voting began President F. W. de Klerk, without Mandela's knowledge, signed a very large portion of land into the trust of Goodwill Zwelithini, the Zulu King.

This very large portion amounted to three million hectares and was all the land controlled by the kwaZulu Legislative Assembly, which body would disappear under the new constitution. Effectively it meant that all the land that was kwaZulu was no longer state land and could not be touched by the new regional government.

Despite all the furore this created in the media when it was discovered in May, I have been told repeatedly since then that if this was the price of averting an escalation in the 'Natal wars' then it was not a big price to pay. I have been told of huts filled with assegais and of huts filled with automatic rifles and of warriors as ready to take hold of their guns as they were to cast their vote. This has been the way people described it, these were the images they conjured up. Always there was the underlying threat of violence.

Of course the violence is still with us. These winter days are filled with it. My copies of the *Weekly Mail & Guardian* show photographs of youths carrying AKs ducking between the houses of Thokoza. They look similar to the photographs by which I understand Rwanda or Bosnia or Somalia or any other place in the world that is said to be at war. But we are not at war; at least, I do not think we are at war. Perhaps if I lived in Thokoza I would think differently. What I am beginning to realize ever more clearly is that we are at peace and at war simultaneously. This is our condition. It is not one or the other.

In my newspaper I can read this:

On the day of the funeral, emotions in the village, fifteen kilometres from Pietersburg, were running high: rumours had spread that Sinna Mankwane, the wife of a small building contractor had bewitched Rasemola. Crowds gathered outside the Mankwane household chanting and demanding that Sinna appear.

As she emerged from her front gate, the mob seized her, beat her and hung three petrol-filled tyres round her neck. Her husband, Johannes, was called out and given a box of matches. In full view of his son and daughter, he was forced to burn his wife alive.

Two days later, as family members gathered at the Mankwane household to pay their respects, the mob returned.

Over the next thirty minutes, Johannes was doused with petrol and burnt alive in his house, while his daughter Martha was stoned and had pieces of wood forced into her vagina before being necklaced. Her brother Frank, who was returning from the village store, was necklaced five hundred metres from where his sister had been murdered.

And over the page I can read about strict gun-control measures being proposed and how well Zwelithini and Mandela get on together and about the appointment of the President of the Constitutional Court and about the millions of rands budgeted for schooling and about how a black consortium has bought fifty-one per cent of a major insurance company.

On the one hand. On the other hand.

The difficulty of living with this dichotomy is that the violence starts to become meaningless. It permeates and perverts the way we think of one another. It destroys the social contract that binds us. There is too much of it. It is too horrible to understand. Consequently the vocabulary used to describe the violence becomes devalued and we no longer allow the mental picture of a person being necklaced to be summoned up by the word. We read it quickly and we do not pause to think of the life taken and how that life ended. I think that if we are to regain our humanity then we have to reinvest these words with the meaning they should carry. And I think the only way to do this is to focus carefully, exactly and constantly on the way people kill and the way people die.

When Bloomsbury received the manuscript of my novel *Horseman* they were appalled by the violence which was, I hope, graphically told and ever-present. It was too much for the reader, they felt; a response elicited from other publishing houses as well. David Philip in South Africa said he had never expected such a book to come out of this country. He said you needed a strong stomach to read it. I thought you needed a strong stomach to live in South Africa. Bloomsbury, however, accepted it, but they still wanted to know what my intention was. And although I thought my intention was obvious I wrote back to tell them I was trying to show what words like 'killing' and 'brutal' and 'hate' and 'revenge' and 'misery' meant. And that they could only regain their meaning if they were depicted without gloss. I have been warned that the effect of such books may cause concerned people in other nations to disregard Africa. But this is wilfully to misread these works. Such books are not retelling colonial stories of the dark continent, they are describing nations in extreme turmoil and distress. They show humanity at its most desperate. They are about suffering. They are pleas for compassion. They attempt to show how violence has become so generalized that we do not understand it until it is rendered in detailed language about a specific event. The specific event is something we cannot escape; we have to confront it and take it into our lives. Through it we learn the meaning of agony.

There were two events which both occurred in December 1993 and which for me were specific moments redolent of our recent times. They told about pain and the nature of some people's delusion, and by responding to them the vocabulary we use to describe violence can be reinvested with moral force. The first was an illegal AWB roadblock in the Western Transvaal which lead to execution-style killings and a grotesque mutilation; the other has become known as the Heidelberg pub massacre. By telling them I hope to show what it is to live here.

6

The AWB roadblock was set up on the night of 13 December 1993 at a crossroads in the mielie fields between Randfontein and Ventersdorp in the Western Transvaal, about forty-five minutes' drive from Johannesburg. Four people died there. One had his ear cut off before he died.

Two months later, towards the end of February 1994, I drove along that road and stopped at the intersection. I left the car on the gravel shoulder and walked about where the people must have been made to sit and where some had been killed. There were no signs of what had happened. Always the worst of what we do can be so quickly wiped away. All that was left was the wind rattling in the eucalyptus trees and stirring through the tall roadside grass where the cosmos was beginning to flower pink and white. I looked at the green mielie fields which filled the horizon. After years of drought the rains had come in abundance and the crop was good. Even at the end of summer the sky was still grey with this intention. Hot and electric and grey. When it rains on such afternoons the air and the ground turn liquid and the red earth runs in the gullies as if blood is being leached from the land.

What occurred on that night in December is now a matter of court record. Simon Nkompone, Teboho Makhuza, Theo

More and eleven-year-old Patrick Gasemane were killed. Petrus and Abrahm Mothupi and William Segotsane will live for the rest of their time with the scars on their bodies and in their minds. Their tormentors and murderers, Petrus Matthews, Martinus van der Schyff, Frederick Badenhorst, Marius Visser and Karel Meiring, all in their twenties, and thirty-nine-year-old André Visser, have been sentenced to death. Two others, Phillipus Cornelius Kloppers and Deon Martin, requested psychological evaluation but a month later were also sentenced to death.

'The callousness of the murders [*sic*] so comprehensively overshadows the possibility of their rehabilitation that the death sentence is the only appropriate sentence,' the judge told the two.

The eight men banded together to carry out AWB leader Eugene Terre'Blanche's injunction to his followers to arm themselves with weapons and prepare themselves for war. They drank some brandies and planned how best to do this. The answer came to them that they should set up a roadblock and stop the free movement of the enemy about the countryside. So they went out to the Redora intersection, placed flashing blue lights on the tops of their cars and stood in the road with torches and automatic rifles. They stopped a minibus-taxi.

'*Is julle ANC?*' they demanded, shining the torches into the frightened faces.

'No,' said the occupants, 'we're not ANC.'

But they were made to get out and sit on the side of the road anyhow. More cars were stopped. The line of those sitting pensively, knowing the nearness of death, lengthened. Kloppers walked up and down before them, occasionally tapping one on the head with his baton.

Then Abrahm and Petrus Mothupi drew up. Things were starting to come apart now. The AWB men did not know what to do with the people. They were edgy and shouting at one another and swinging their guns about wildly. They ordered Petrus Mothupi out of the car and as he climbed out someone hit him, and that persuaded Abrahm Mothupi that he should not move.

The men yelled at him to get out.

But he would not.

They screamed at him.

But he would not move.

One of them shot him in the face.

Some of the captives started to run, fleeing into the fields of young crops.

'Don't just stand there,' Martin shouted at the commandos, 'shoot!'

And Teboho Makhuza and Patrick Gasemane were shot as they fled. And Theo More had a gun put to the back of his head and was executed for the crime of being black and being on that road that night. And Simon Nkompone was stabbed repeatedly as he tried to hide in a car.

Then Kloppers may or may not have ordered Martin to 'Take his ear,' who did anyhow, using his hunting knife to mutilate Nkompone while the man was still alive. This done, Martin wiped his blade on Petrus Mothupi, who was feigning death beside a burning car.

Martin offered the ear to Kloppers, who said, 'What the fuck is that?' but took it none the less and later, when they were drinking more brandies at Frederick Badenhorst's house, held it up saying, 'Look what I have.'

In court Martin said of his deed: 'I'm talking about something that gives me nightmares. It seemed to me he was dead. I cannot believe I did such a thing.'

Simon Nkompone died three days after the attack.

On the day they were sentenced in the Johannesburg Supreme Court a reporter wrote: 'Most of the accused looked jovial and often mocking. None looked directly at the relatives of those they had shot execution-style. Only one, whose lanky black hair flopped over his forehead seemed reflective and ashamed. He sat apart from the others in a cream suit and striped tie.'

In passing sentence the judge said, 'Their goal was simply to kill. Their regret is not expressed in their actions after the murder nor in their actions in court. They have displayed no real remorse – it appears to us they are not concerned about the consequences their actions have for them. Their blatant racist behaviour led them to assault and murder. If this behaviour goes unpunished a pattern of crime and violence will continue.'

Softly, naming no names, he read out the numbers of those to be hanged: 1, 2, 3, 4, 5 and 8. Each was given four death sentences.

I was on the road to Ventersdorp that afternoon in February to get a story about teenage love in the right wing. A New York magazine was planning a series on true romance in times of civil war. They were going to have dispatches from Bosnia and Northern Ireland and Somalia and wherever else they felt events fitted their reality. Once again there rose that question: were we involved in a civil war? No, not in Muizenberg. But yes, in places in Natal and in places on the East Rand. In Thokoza I could have got them a story matching bullet for bullet the one they had received from Sarajevo. But I had talked them into considering something different: something that was not civil war but a state of siege. Something that was created by propaganda and make-believe in the bar of the Ventersdorp hotel and by paranoia in farmhouses. They had agreed. But I was uneasy, suspecting that what I wrote would not fit the pattern in their minds.

Thirty kilometres before Ventersdorp a placard stuck on a roadsign read: HIER BEGIN ONS VOLKSTAAT. It meant I was now entering one of the nebulous right-wing national states. But the Afrikaans words were loaded. They told of defiance and fear and racism. They told of a small group of people at odds with the world, frightened by history, clinging desperately to a brief time when their way was law. I looked at their *volkstaat*. I saw mielie fields and power-lines and some black schoolchildren walking along the side of the road. Nearer to the dorp I saw black men driving tractors on the land and black people cycling to the shops. In the dorp itself I saw no whites. The first whites I saw were in the Christian bookshop, where I went to ask directions to the school. There were four of them. Two saleswomen and two women buying Bibles. I was given directions and, to my query, was told they sold three to four Bibles a day. There are some five thousand souls in Ventersdorp and the nearby township of Tshing. It seemed to me they had a good business.

Back in the car I wondered what biblical passages were being read. I got an answer, of sorts, in the beautiful Dutch Reformed church that dominates the surrounding buildings. The doors were unlocked, a cleaner was dusting up at what Philip Larkin called 'the holy end'. On a board listing some hymn numbers was a reference to Isaiah, chapter 1, verses 24 to 28. Days later I looked them up:

24 Therefore saith the Lord, the Lord of hosts, the mighty One of Israel, Ah, I will ease me of mine adversaries, and avenge me of mine enemies:
25 And I will turn my hand upon thee, and purely purge away thy dross, and take away all thy tin:
26 And I will restore thy judges as at the first, and thy counsellors as at the beginning: afterward thou shalt be called, The city of righteousness, the faithful city.

27 Zion shall be redeemed with judgment, and her converts with righteousness.

28 And the destruction of the transgressors and of the sinners shall be together, and they that forsake the Lord shall be consumed.

In those pre-election days the small Western Transvaal town of Ventersdorp was one of the 'capitals' of the longed-for *volkstaat*. At the town's entrance the independence flag that rallied the Boer commandos during the Anglo-Boer War almost a century ago proclaimed the town's status. The flagpole was fringed in barbed wire; the flag hung limply in the rumbling air.

It was a decrepit town. The shops on the main road had broken windows, decaying plasterwork and dull façades that had not been painted in a long time. It was a town without a cinema, without a disco, without a pool hall, without a video arcade. It was a mean and tatty dorp.

Yet surprisingly Ventersdorp's residential area was well kept: the lawns mown, the houses neat and painted. Some were tightly barricaded with high fences crowned in razor wire, but others were unfenced and opened directly on to the quiet, empty streets. Outwardly it was a peaceful dorp in the middle of the maize belt. But inside the heads of many in this town were feelings of betrayal, alienation, anger, fear, and a growing belief that their only recourse to thwart black rule was through violence.

Ventersdorp had nothing to offer young people except a school, a church and a less obvious form of activity that took place on some select farms in the surrounding districts. These exercises in what was termed 'self-defence' were not exactly covert, but they were not exactly overt either. Unless you were part of the cell you wouldn't know they were going on.

In one of these houses lived AWB Commandant Sannie,

who said she kept a 'beautiful gun' in her kitchen, ever ready for the call to arms that the crossroads murderers had already heeded. In others lived commandos who would be equally armed and equally convinced they were in a state of siege that would soon develop into a full-scale civil war.

They did not need to live in bullet-pocked houses, nor risk their lives every time they went out to buy bread, to know they were at war. There did not have to be snipers in the streets; there did not have to be incoming mortarfire to convince them that war was none the less upon them.

Because of their siege mentality, it was difficult to talk freely to the young people in the dorp. Sannie would not hear of it.

'No,' she said, 'you are not talking to my children. When they're living out of this house they can say what they like, but while they stay here I talk for them.'

The school headmaster had similar views. He had issued instructions that no pupils were to talk to the press unless he or their parents were present. I found this out when I approached a group of girls sitting on the grass outside a hostel. They told me very quickly about the headmaster's rule.

'*Meneer moet met Meneer Looke praat,*' they said.

I did not want to talk to Meneer Looke. I could see no point in talking to Meneer Looke, but even so I went to see him. His wife opened the door. I felt like a schoolboy ordered to report to the headmaster. I explained myself. She listened, saying 'Ja' like a full stop at the end of my sentences.

When I had finished she said, 'Why do you people always pick on Ventersdorp? We're just ordinary people here in Ventersdorp. But you people make this town seem like something bad where we hate the blacks. But we're not like that, we're just ordinary people here.' (A few weeks later these ordinary people would detonate a large bomb in Tshing.)

Her husband appeared from a back room, barefoot, wearing a pair of black rugby shorts and a white shirt with the sleeves rolled up, the collar unbuttoned. He blinked in the harsh light. He had been watching cricket on television.

He had heard my stammered, incoherent request. He had heard his wife's reply. He blinked at me. Invited me in. We went through to a sitting room and sat on heavy chairs with wooden armrests. His wife did not join us. Once more I had to relay my assignment.

He thought about what I said for a long time. He looked up at the wall. His head rested lightly on his right hand. His small finger lay across his lips. The silence went on and on. The cricket commentary had been turned down.

Eventually he said that if I came back the next day he would have selected three pupils for me to talk to and would have obtained their parents' permission. That was the best he could do. He clasped his hands with finality. It was the better of the two scenarios I had predicted but it was still no good. I thanked him and left.

I drove back to the main street, defeated, at a loss.

Sitting at a table outside what must once have been a roadhouse but was now closed and boarded up, reduced to a small shop, a hole in the wall without a window that sold soft drinks, cigarettes, packets of potato crisps, newspapers and photo-romances, were five teenagers. They were still in their school uniforms: the boys' ties were slightly askew, the girls' gymslips had been hitched a bit higher than regulations probably stipulated.

I bought a Coke and approached them. I asked disingenuously what they did for fun in a dorp like this. They laughed and squirmed with embarrassment and said not much. Then admitted that sometimes they went to Potchef-stroom, a nearby town with cinemas and steakhouses and clubs. But they could only do that if someone with a driver's licence could borrow a car to get them there. We started talking.

The five were Elsabet, Piet, Anna, Hannes and Beverly. Elsabet was sixteen years old. She had a boyfriend who believed that 'the *swartes*' would never rule the country.

'My boyfriend says Mandela will never be our pres-ident,' were her words.

The others agreed.

'He says we'll fight them until they give us our own country.'

'That's what my father says,' added Piet. 'This is our country. This is where the voortrekkers came and settled.'

'Ja,' put in Hannes, 'there were no blacks living here then so how can they take it away from us?'

I wanted to know how they planned to resist majority rule when they were a minority.

'We can shoot,' said Elsabet. 'We know how.'

I asked if they had learned to shoot at school.

Anna shook her head. Hannes smiled. Piet bit his lip. Beverly and Elsabet giggled.

'Where then?' I persisted.

'With Elsabet's boyfriend,' said Beverly.

'Don't tell,' said Elsabet, but there was something defiant in her attitude. 'We are just as good as the boys,' she boast-ed. She was referring to their prowess in handling guns.

'Ja?'

'Ja.'

'Where did you meet your boyfriend?'

'At a church braaivleis. Sometimes there's also a band and we can dance. But it's not disco.' They all laughed. 'Just *sakkie-sakkie*' – a traditional Afrikaner waltz.

She explained that Paul, her boyfriend, was nineteen years old, had finished school and had a driving licence. He worked on his father's farm just outside the dorp. Sometimes he fetched her to go shooting on the farm.

'You mean hunting?'

Elsabet giggled: 'No, man, shooting at targets.'

But we had now been talking for too long and the shopkeeper was watching us from the doorway. She called to Elsabet, who went inside and did not come out again. The woman approached us. She told the youngsters to go home, said that Elsabet had to finish her homework. She asked me if there was anything more I wanted.

I shook my head. She went back to her shop doorway, and I drove off to the Magaliesberg to spend the night with friends whose family had farmed in the mountains for almost a hundred years. My heart was singing at this unexpected success. I drove fast. On the radio a journalist was discussing the types of bullet-proof jackets available to the media. The best one was predictably the most expensive. But it had been tried and tested in Bosnia.

I switched off the radio. I did not want to listen to the merits of various makes of bullet-proof jackets or why they were necessary. My light-hearted mood had gone. I heard again the words of Elsabet: 'We'll fight them until they give us our own country. Mandela will never be our president.' She was so sure of herself. They were all so sure of themselves. Their world was fixed: determined by what their parents said and what their friends said and probably what their teachers said. And they did not question it because they could not imagine any other world. Their way was right, morally right, because they believed it was ordained by God and history. Yet they were also ordinary teenagers. At a Potchefstroom disco there would be nothing about them that spoke of an ability to shoot handguns or semi-automatics. Or even an ability like Frederick Badenhorst and André Visser, who were just a year or two older than Elsabet's boyfriend, to kill. Were they really going to start a mean internecine war after the elections?

The paramilitary exercises Elsabet hinted at have been well documented in the newspapers. The photographs, often taken at some risk, show khaki-clad men and women and children bearing the AWB's swastika-like insignia on their armbands, marching in platoons, or flat on the ground firing at distant targets. But there are also photographs of these commandos relaxing round the braaivleis fires afterwards: cooking meat, drinking brandies mixed with Coke, laughing. And of youngsters dancing to music being squashed out by an accordion player.

A figure frequently seen at these clandestine gatherings and at more blatant propaganda meetings in the dorps and bigger towns is Marguerite Vermeulen of an international neo-Nazi organization known by the acronym WAM – World Apartheid Movement. She usually sports rings and bangles with her close-fitting khaki uniform and is intent on teaching young people, particularly women, a lethal form of self-defence. WAM's message is that decent folk have become the prey of the lawless masses and have to defend themselves if Christian morality is to continue holding sway in the world.

'Of course young people come to me,' she is quoted as saying. 'I offer them a place and a time when they can be together. I teach them how to think positively, and I teach them how to take care of themselves.'

Vermeulen is especially strong on rape. But rape is merely a rallying cry in what she sees as an intensifying racial war. Her ideas on rape have less to do with men than with black power and dominance.

'Rape is a weapon in a war which has never been declared,' she has said. She will then hold up a poster showing a gorilla and a black man. Beneath the photographs is the question: *What is the difference?* Beneath that is this answer: *The gorilla will neither attack you, nor will it give you AIDS.*

'I teach young girls how to kill a rapist by snapping his neck to the side, even if he has pinned her to the ground,' she once told a reporter. 'If I can teach every woman this South American technique there'd be no rape.'

In the month before the elections, Ventersdorp celebrated the maize harvest with a festival. They do so every year. I was not there but I imagine Vermeulen was, with her tent full of propaganda. The AWB commandos would have been strutting around in their uniforms and among them would have been Paul, holding Elsabet's hand. Her friends would have been there too, Hannes and Piet and Anna and Beverly and probably most of the other youngsters from the dorp. Around the braaivleis fires there would have been talk of the coming dark days and the prayers and Lord's strength they would need to get them through. Then the accordion player would sound his notes and the dancing would begin. And for a while young and old would have lost their paranoia in the emotion of the dance as they swept round and round in the arms of those they loved.

The Magaliesberg farm I was headed towards belonged to Terence and Marge. I had been friends with their family since the late Sixties when we lived in the same Johannesburg suburb. Their son Derek and I shared a quest: the search for the perfect way to cook lobster.

Over the years I had come to hold their farm as a cherished place, a place that could be summoned quietly into the mind when the world turned rough. It is a place of great hospitality and long nights of *mampoer* – the clear moonshine liquor brewed in the vicinity. In the dim *voorkamer* there are deep couches for those who wish to drink and discuss politics and even examine the nature of their souls. Because those who drink *mampoer* will be there for a long time and their conversation will become quite intricate. And if they are still there on the couches when the sun rises, then they are grateful that the stoep is wide and the front room dim.

In a cabinet in the *voorkamer* there are bottles with handwritten labels distinguishing the peach *mampoer* from the plum, the apple from the orange. They all taste the same. They all work in the same subtle way. After a few hours drinking *mampoer* you are nothing but a talking head. You certainly cannot shift your legs. And it is only the constant movement of your hand taking the glass from the chair's armrest to your mouth that has prevented it from becoming as numb as your other limbs.

Mampoer is a very sociable drink: it stimulates conversation, encourages debate, keeps the participants involved, and when tempers flare it renders those who would normally reach for their guns inactive. It has other, more mystical properties too.

I sat in the *voorkamer* one evening at the height of P. W. Botha's state of emergency in the Eighties drinking *mampoer* with Derek, and there came a time when the house was still and the veld was as quiet and we paused in our words to take a drink and at that moment the horses of the apocalypse ridden by silent Maleficents thundered about the farmhouse and passed on. Derek and I nodded sagely at the darkness of the times we lived in. Soon his father came stumbling through, muttering that the horses had got loose again, but we warned him that matters were far graver.

The farm is at the foot of the Magaliesberg Mountain. It is at the end of a road that will wipe the sump off any car too recklessly driven. There are four stick-and-wire gates that have to be opened and closed as the road becomes a track, as the sense of going into the bush increases. And finally there is an approach across a piece of flat land where the grass is tall and yellow and once ran with guineafowl. But they were poached in the last months of 1993: both a warning to the white farmer and a measure of local need.

Despite the attacks on neighbouring farms Terence and Marge live without concessions to the times except that they are now linked by radio to a cell of nearby farmers. They live in what is known as a Red Alert Area, which seems to mean that there will be an armed response at the merest alarm. Yet they are not protected by high electric fences of razor wire. There are no floodlights. The nights are as dark as nights have ever been. There are no pit-bull terriers lying in wait in the deep shadows of the stoep. Terence is armed: he has hunting rifles, but farmers always have hunting rifles. He could have drawn an R1 automatic rifle for himself and a handgun for Marge from the local police station but he could not see the point.

He joked that after the elections the ANC would go through the lists of farmers who had R1s, and those would be the first farms they would reallocate to people who had been dispossessed of land.

Perhaps most nights they now lock the external doors, but sometimes they forget and sometimes they cannot be bothered.

At seven Terence radioed the other farmers in the cell. He made arrangements to have dinner with one; and asked another if he would call round to repair their leaking roof. A third said he would be burning firebreaks higher up the mountain in the coming days and Terence said he would send some men to help him. A fourth said his wife was still ill but the doctor had prescribed stronger medicine. 'Give her our regards,' said Terence as he signed off.

After dinner he told me about the AWB in the area. They were going to fight, he said. They felt betrayed and angry and afraid. Some probably had weapons stockpiled on their farms and some had taken loans to buy extra ammunition for their rifles. One man said he had extended his overdraft facilities by R7,000 to do just that.

'You must understand,' he said, 'they don't see things the way we do. A kaffir is a kaffir to them. He's a savage who if the whites weren't here would sit under a tree all day and let the women till the fields. These people have got no time for blacks. They just don't see things the way we do.'

To Terence the way we saw things was that the ANC had a legitimate call to government and a mandate to straighten out the years of apartheid. He could get vociferous about this: earnest and appalled at the way things had been.

I slept in the outside room that night. It smelled faintly of insecticide or fertilizer or how I imagined insecticide or fertilizer should smell. It was the sort of room one should sleep in on a farm: a room of strange strips of leather and forgotten tins and a basin with a dark brown stain where the tap dripped. I was tired yet I could not sleep. I had not drunk any *mampoer* because I wanted to be able to see the next morning and I did not want to be visited by any passing Maleficents. But perhaps a single *mampoer* would have slipped me over the edge. Soon the mosquitoes found me and I tried to slap them on my face and regretted not packing my insect repellent. I pulled the sheet over my head.

Instead of counting sheep I began to play out an imaginary soap opera in the hope that it would send me to sleep. It was the story of Elsa and Koos.

Elsa was a schoolgirl with hair that was never quite clean and a pallor to her skin that resembled day-old white bread. She chewed her nails. Her face was thin and there was in her eyes a softness that appealed for love and a quickness that might have been fear.

Her family had been AWB members since the movement's inception during the 1980s. Her father was a commandant in charge of twenty men. Her brother was in the commando. Her mother, like many Afrikaner women of her generation, supported her menfolk in whatever they did.

Elsa's family lived at Ventersdorp. Their house was surrounded by a tall wire fence that opened in a V at the top to support coils of razor wire. A fringe of razor wire hung from the roof and there was some rolled strategically over the chimney. Elaborate burglar bars glistened at the windows; a security grille protected the front door. Beneath a mimosa tree lay a Rottweiler. Its turds littered the lawn; it had dug up the garden in boredom.

Koos was an apprentice mechanic on the gold mines. He had a straggly blond moustache and his hair was too long for his small head. When he spoke he had a curious way of jerking his chin, as if challenging the listener to deny what he said. Koos was not politically motivated. When his friends invited him to an AWB braai at Ventersdorp he went because it was something to do on an empty Saturday afternoon. He was twenty years old and the weekends could be tedious.

But at Ventersdorp, on a night towards the end of summer, when jaggers of lightning played along the horizon and the laughter of the khaki-clad people swirled around him, Koos was seduced by the aroma of cooking meat on the heavy air and the accordion music tapping in his foot. When Elsa appeared out of the braai smoke bearing a plate of sausage rolls he asked her to dance. They did not speak while they danced, but afterwards they held hands and, in the darkness, kissed.

Koos went home with Elsa's telephone number scrawled on a paper serviette.

Because of the distance between their towns, their romance grew slowly. But after his fifth visit her father asked her if Koos was a member of the AWB.

'We are an AWB family,' he said. 'We don't want fence-sitters here. So you better find out about him because he's not welcome any more unless he's one of us.'

'OK,' said Koos, when Elsa asked him. 'I'll join because they're doing some good things.'

So Koos joined. But joining was not enough. Next Elsa's father insisted he accompany the commando on a 'camp'.

Koos did not want to go but he had no choice.

And one winter's weekend Koos found himself at a camp in the thorn-veld on a farm near the country's northern border. He had changed his civilian clothes for a khaki uniform with the AWB's swastika-like insignia on the armbands. During the day he learned to fire an automatic rifle; during the night he stalked through the veld playing a war game with guns that fired bullets of paint. It was not something that Koos enjoyed. He went on two more of these camps before the police arrested him during a general round-up of right-wing activists. Bombs had gone off in the region, sabotaging power-lines and buildings. And the politicians wanted it stopped.

They released him the same day but Koos was frightened. He phoned Elsa. He spoke so softly she could hardly hear him.

'This is not nice,' he told her. 'I'm frightened, kookie. I mean, how did they even know I was AWB? They told me it was long years of jail if they caught us. And the rope for sure if someone died. It's not nice, kookie.'

He told her he was catching the bus to Cape Town to get away from all the trouble. She cried and pleaded but Koos was too frightened to be swayed by love. He went, and a few months later she ran away from home to join him.

I imagined them living in a grim flat near the railway with a view over a cemetery. Koos had found work in a local vehicle-repair shop; Elsa did not have a job. Every night they would sit in the only two chairs they possessed and watch television. When the programmes ended they would go to sleep on their mattress upon the floor.

It was a true soap. I could hear the accordion music of the signature tune. I fell asleep as the notes drifted away.

Sometime later a scream tore into my sleep. It was a pitch of scream a Maleficent would howl as it towered up to exact revenge. In fright I yelled back, but the screeching continued in the blackness above my head.

Gradually the scream ended, going down into a chittering. I lay tensed, hardly breathing, listening. The room was completely silent. Then it screamed again. The light switch was on a farther wall but I preferred to stay in the dark. I waited, trying to pick out the scratch of clawed feet across the beams. But there was no sound beyond the thump of my heart. When it screamed for the third time the noise came from another part of the room. It did not call again. I lay thinking about Elsa and Koos in their flat above the railyards where the goods trains were shunted and coupled before dawn.

The next morning Marge said, 'Did you sleep well?'

I told her about the screaming.

'The screaming!' She looked quizzically at me. 'Oh, you mean the bushbaby. I am sorry. We should have told you about the bushbaby.'

Back in Johannesburg, in the student cafeteria of the Rand Afrikaans University, I spoke to Niels, who told a poignant story of unrequited love. Niels laughed and smoked a lot. He had a broad face that hid no secrets. He would draw on the cigarette and let the smoke trickle out of his nose and watch me to see how I accepted his more candid revelations. He enjoyed his story. He embellished it. Probably he thought it was a good joke. If he had not set his heart on building bridges he could have become an actor.

'Half an hour before we were attacked I tiptoed into Susanna's bedroom,' he began. 'It wasn't the first time. I'd done it every night I'd been there, and I'd been there a week by then. It was a new house with carpets so it was easy. There were no wooden floorboards to creak and wake up her parents. All I had to worry about was whether the dog was going to bark. But I made friends with him early on. Even so I was shit-scared that her dad would hear the door hinges squeak. You've no idea how much noise a door hinge makes in the middle of the night. I was worried about him. He would have beaten the shit out of me. No questions and straight home on the next train.

'It was the first time I'd visited their farm. Susanna and I had been going steady for about six months, since school started that year anyhow. And then for the winter holidays she said why didn't I come out to the farm and I couldn't say yes quickly enough.

'So there I was, pushing her bedroom door closed and letting the door handle go very slowly so it wouldn't make any noise. It was bloody cold. I was shivering from the cold and probably from excitement. All I was wearing was a tracksuit.

'Susanna was a pain. She wouldn't let me get under the duvet and I had to lie there on the top of the bed with my feet like ice. No matter how much I pleaded with her she wouldn't let me get into the bed. So we lay there kissing and such.'

Niels laughed at the image. He had not shaved for a few days and when light caught the stubble his cheeks glowed in soft focus. He thought he had sketched an enormously funny picture.

'Let me tell you first about the house. You see, it wasn't the first time they'd been attacked. The first time was in January. They came one night and fired shots at the house and then disappeared into the mountains. No one was hurt but it gave her parents a fright. They got electric fencing and floodlights and big dogs that were unchained each night in the garden. Those dogs, Rottweilers I think, were trained to attack. You didn't mess around with them. Not like Frikkie inside the house. Frikkie was a Dobermann, but quite a stupid dog.

'Also Susanna's father got two R1 rifles from the police and a .38 pistol. He already had a shotgun and a hunting rifle and a small revolver but he didn't think that was much use against AKs. When Susanna's mother was alone in the house she wore the pistol strapped to her waist. The police taught her how to use it and the R1. She even let us use it to shoot tin cans in the veld. She thought it was just as well that Susanna and her brother learned to shoot.'

I should add that, between the first attack on Susanna's

farm and the second, five other farmsteads in the Ficksburg district near the Lesotho border were shot up. In the fourth incident a couple in their seventies were killed in their beds. To the farmers this was a declaration of war. But the enemy was invisible. Its soldiers could rank among their labourers or they could be trained men infiltrating from the nearby mountains. It was a state of siege that was intensified by a feeling of vulnerability. The constant fear gave rise to a paranoia that bred in the families like a disease.

'You could see it in them all the time,' said Niels. 'They just didn't know what was going to happen next. They tried to live like normal people but you can't live like normal people when you've got all that security. It didn't bother me. I was just there for a holiday. But I couldn't have lived like that day after day.'

He lit another cigarette.

'Tell me about the attack.'

'Ja.' Ropes of smoke curled out of his nose and threaded upwards. 'Ja. In a way it was funny but it was also fucking terrifying. I mean there I was, more worried about how I'm going to get back to my bedroom than about the bullets. Susanna was screaming because her window had shattered and the glass was all over the bed. They had thrown a Molotov cocktail through the sitting-room window and it had burst into flames. They were shooting at us and Susanna's father was shooting at them with the R1 and I was trying to get back to my bedroom on the other side of the passageway.

'Next thing Susanna's father was shouting at me to go and put out the flames and then I realized that he didn't know anything. He thought I'd just come out of my room. I was so grateful I went and beat out the flames with a cushion. It wasn't much of a fire anyhow. By now the shooting had stopped. But I was shaking. I just couldn't stop shaking.'

Niels smiled.

'That was the end. Full stop. Finish and *klaar*. The next morning she wouldn't speak to me, she wouldn't let me touch her. Her mother said she was in shock and it would be best if I went home. She was at school for the rest of the year but she didn't want to have anything to do with me.

'You see, in a way, I think she felt maybe I was to blame. I think she thought that by lying together we had sinned. I don't know. Maybe she even thought it was a sort of punishment. Her family was very religious. Her father said prayers at each mealtime and I think he used to read a passage from the Bible aloud to her mother each evening before they went to sleep.

'There are probably some girls here,' he waved an arm around the cafeteria, 'who would have done the same thing; but I think she was a bit screwed up with all the Dutch Reformed Church teachings.'

'Do you know what's happened to her?'

'No.' He shook his head. 'I think maybe she's at university in the Cape. Maybe she's less uptight now that things aren't so bad in her parents' part of the country.'

In these days the right wing has been quiet. Who can tell when they will resort to another spate of bombings? That they will perpetrate some further violence is inevitable and may be a legacy that will live on in our history for some generations yet. I often think of Elsabet and her boyfriend Paul and her other friends and wonder how they have adapted to the change which just five months ago they could not contemplate. For all I know, one of them may one day plant a car-bomb. But in the mean time nothing will have changed in their day-to-day lives. They will still need Paul's car to get them to the disco in Potchefstroom. They will still be buying tapes of grunge music and dancing the *sakkie-sakkie* at church braais. And maybe they will begin to realize that the story they have been told about the world has some weird parts to it.

7

The second atrocity I want to tell was perpetrated by the PAC at the end of December 1993. There is no meaningful sense in which the one event is connected to the other; perhaps the most that can be said about them is that they describe us at moments of hate, self-loathing and fear. In this they are no different to all the other outbreaks of horror in the country; but the PAC's action shocked because it was so near.

The question I asked on the morning of 31 December while Jill and I listened to the news was: what whim of fate had made us drive on? We looked at one another across the security of the muesli and the yoghurt and the fruit and both thought: That could have been us! By minutes that could have been us! But it was not. We were alive. Four were dead; three were wounded, one of whom would probably never walk again. Such news puckered the flesh and brought a sombreness to the day.

We telephoned the friends we had been with the night before.

'A close one,' said Bruce. 'Just a few minutes later and . . .'

The rest did not bear thinking about.

Because minutes before it happened we had left the

Africa Café flushed with the exuberance of the evening and the bite of the chilli sauce, driven slowly down Lower Main Road, Observatory, and stopped at the traffic lights at the Station Road intersection. Next to us was the Heidelberg Tavern. The laughter and the voices of the drinkers sounded into the street.

'Come on, one last drink,' someone suggested.

'Shall we?'

'Yes, come on.'

'No. It's late. It's time for bed.'

'It's not even midnight.'

'That's late. Long past bedtime.'

And that decided it. The traffic light changed to green and we turned into Station Road and drove slowly past the houses my great-grandfather had built so much earlier in the century, up towards the mountain looming above the lights.

Station Road is a narrow one-way street. That night, 30 December, cars were parked haphazardly along the kerbs on both sides of the road. I now wonder, was one of those cars an orange *bakkie*, with men sitting in it waiting? Or was it perhaps the car that flashed its lights, signalling us on while they politely waited, aware that they were driving the wrong way down the street? I shall never know. All I know is that moments after we turned out of Station Road an orange *bakkie* stopped outside the Heidelberg Tavern and four masked men carrying R4 rifles got out.

What happened next can be written in fifty words. In the words are death and carnage and shattered lives that will be shattered for ever. In the words is a violence which should not be forgotten just as those who did it should not be forgiven.

A *bakkie* stops and four masked men carrying R4 rifles get out. They shoot at people on the pavement outside the pub. Then go inside and fire two long bursts into the crowded room. As they leave one drops a grenade spiked with nails into the bodies and the silence.

The grenade came to rest a short distance from the head of twenty-year-old Quentin Cornelius, who had arrived on holiday from Johannesburg that afternoon. He was lying beneath a bench. He had been shot in the back and the bullet had ripped through him and left a hole in his stomach. As he lay there he could feel his intestines oozing out of the hole. He turned to look at the grenade but it did not interest him: his pain was too great to admit fear.

Steve Hamilton had gone into the pub to buy some cigarettes. He was waiting for his change when, as he put it, 'all hell broke loose'. 'I ducked behind a pillar and hit the deck. I couldn't see the attackers but when the gunfire started I looked towards the entrance and saw two girls fly like puppets off their feet. When people realized what was happening some dived under tables but others seemed too numb to move and just flopped down on the spot and lay still like rag dolls. The shots lasted for a minute and were fired in two bursts. After the firing there was a deathly silence. The bar was clouded with smoke, there were people lying everywhere. Others were walking around, dazed, shocked.'

Mike Ross was sitting at the back of the room. 'The shots seemed to go on for ever,' he told a reporter. 'People were screaming and turning tables over. I ran over to see some women near the front and saw that two were dead. But there was a third woman near them who was struggling to breathe so I lifted her up slightly and held her in my arms. She was in a bad way. There was nothing I could do and when her head flopped back I knew it was over.'

Michael January and his cousin Grant January went into the pub for a quick drink ten minutes before the attack. Michael was shot in the leg. Grant was wounded by flying splinters of glass. As Michael's mother told a *Cape Times* reporter: 'They didn't even have time to finish their drinks.' She also said, 'My son had his skull cracked by the police when he protested against the 1983 constitution. Now he is shot by people on the other side. What do you think? What do you do? I am just grateful he is alive.'

David Deglon, a student at the University of Cape Town, was also grateful to be alive. Grateful and angry. He was wounded, but his two flatmates, twenty-three-year-old Lindy-Anne Fourie and twenty-two-year-old Bernadette Langford, were both killed. He told the Mayor when she visited him in hospital: 'We are sick of violence. We have had enough of it.' He told the press: 'It's time these random acts of violence from the left and right came to a stop and we started to work towards peace in this country. I'm obviously shocked, but these sorts of things are happening quite often. I don't really feel much resentment towards the people who did this. I just wish they would stop. We've had enough of violence.'

The other two killed were Joe Cerqueira, who ran a restaurant on the same corner as the Tavern. He was shot in the street. And twenty-two-year-old Rolande Palm, who had recently moved from Durban because she had seen a woman stabbed in the back. She was planning to join the police and work in the child-protection unit. She was with her father in the pub. 'I blame myself for her death,' he told reporters. 'I grabbed her head and tried to bring her to the floor. I felt for her pulse and when I couldn't find it I ran home screaming. She came here because she didn't want to die by the knife or the bullet.' He was unhurt.

On 4 January 1994 the police arrested the PAC's regional chairman Theo Mabusela and the regional organizer Nkosnathi Siyolo. Mabusela had just put the phone down to an SABC television reporter. He had said that if the government persisted in its efforts to victimize the PAC then 1994 would be 'the year of the bullet, not the year of the ballot'.

Some days later three other PAC members were arrested: Richard Madodadala, Brian Madasi and Zola Mabala. And in late August a sixth man, Luyanda Gqumfa, allegedly a member of the PAC's armed wing, APLA, was detained.

In July I sought out Quentin Cornelius, Michael January and Ginn Fourie, the mother of Lindy, to hear their stories, because they were the victims, they were the ones who would be forgotten. The gunmen, if they were found guilty and not sentenced to death, would serve probably no more than a decade in prison and then be rehabilitated by the state. Meanwhile the state was not helping the victims. As Quentin Cornelius said without any self-pity: 'I have already been forgotten. I believe very few people remember what happened.'

I met Quentin Cornelius in a restaurant in Johannesburg. His mother drove him there but he propelled his wheelchair from the car to the table. No heads turned as he entered the restaurant, no eyes followed him, and yet he is a hero. It must be remembered about him that he will never regain the use of his legs below the knees. It must be remembered that he has only one kidney and that his intestines will require intermittent operations to keep them functioning. Above all it must be remembered that he will never be out of pain. He is twenty-one years old.

This is what he said:

If I remember correctly we went to the Heidelberg for a few beers at about quarter-past ten. Lindy [Fourie] and I were sitting with our backs to the door and Dave [Deglon] and Bernie [Bernadette Langford] were opposite us at the table. I was just about to get up and buy another round of beers when I heard the first shots and instinctively I dived for the floor. I had heard machine-gun fire before at cadet camps and I knew instantly that this was automatic fire. It was in this dive that I got caught. The range of fire was right across us. But if I hadn't dived I would have died. Lindy was sitting next to me and she had four shots through her back. I was directly in the line of fire. I am sure I would have been killed if I had sat still.

I remember an incredible amount of pain. Instantly. I could hardly breathe. I was lying under a table and when the shooting stopped it was total chaos. People were ripping the place apart to get out. I remember hearing someone shouting about a grenade. I turned my head and I saw it, but some guy said to me, 'Don't worry, it's not true: they're just trying to get people out of the place.' I didn't think anything more about the grenade: I had too much pain. My hands were starting to go rigid. A guy was holding my hand and kept on screaming in my ear and asking my name. I was very close to just giving up. But he kept on shouting at me, he kept on shaking me and I held his hand. The next day he came to see me in hospital and showed me his hand was bruised blue from the way I had gripped it.

At first people wanted to take me to hospital in a car, but I didn't want anyone to move me as I knew that my back was broken. It seemed that the medical help took for ever to get there yet I was told they were there within ten or so minutes. I was put on to a special stretcher and carried out to the ambulance. I remember camera flash-lights going off all around me.

Once at the hospital I was wheeled into the trauma room. At this time I had become much calmer as I was probably given some injections, which also helped for the worst of the pain. I was left lying in this room for several hours as the initial check-ups showed that all the intest-ines to the right of my spine were completely ripped up. Continuous checks and X-rays were taken to ascertain whether the left kidney was still functioning normally; if not, a transplant would have had to be arranged. In the mean time specialists were called in, and I was eventually taken into the theatre at five-thirty in the morning. Lying in that room for the best part of five hours once again felt like for ever, but at least I was more at ease as I knew that I would be well taken care of now that I was in hospital.

The operation, during which my right kidney, sixty centimetres of my colon and several pieces of small intest-ine were removed and the rest was patched up and put together again, lasted almost six hours.

Obviously during this time I had no idea what had happened to Lindy or Bernie. Sometime the next day, after the operation, I remember waking to find Lindy's father standing next to my bed. I asked him if Lindy was all right. His eyes filled with tears. He told me they had just come from the mortuary. Then I blacked out.

I had terrible dreams during the first weeks but that was also from the morphine. One night it was like I was talking to them, to Lindy and Bernie. It was very difficult coming to accept that they had been killed. You know Lindy's mother works at the hospital. Every morning she came to see me, and I cried every time she visited. It was a terrible experience.

There are days now I feel trapped and get very depressed. Especially the last few weeks during the university holidays. Now I'm dependent on people coming to see me and often I feel I have been rejected and people have forgotten me. I know this is just a perception because I still have lots of friends visiting me. But there are certain days when the pain is immense and it is difficult to cope with it. I am thinking of trying acupuncture or meditation to help me overcome the pain. You see, it is always there. And I am always going to have it. I was on very heavy drugs for months. I became addicted to them twice and had to go back to intensive care to be rehabilitated. I used to ask the doctors when the pain would go away because I couldn't stay on drugs for the rest of my life. They kept on ducking the question: I never got a straight answer. Eventually one of the nurses sat with me on a day I was crying from the pain and she said the reason everybody was avoiding this question was because I was going to have this pain for the rest of my life. She said my pain threshhold would increase and it would be easier to live with, but it was always going to be there. I must admit there are even some days now when I realize I haven't been thinking about the pain, that it hasn't bothered me. But then there are some days when it is so bad that I want to scream. When the nurse told me this I felt a lot of anger. I still battle to accept that I am not independent any more. I was active before. I used to go gliding, cycling, canoeing. I used to play golf. At varsity I was a director of the radio station. All that has come to a stop.

As far as I am concerned those who did it are murderers, they have wrecked people's lives for the rest of their lives and for that they should hang. I want justice to be done. I know it's not going to help me, I know hanging them is not solving anything, but something has to be done. I blame the political situation in South Africa for what happened. If it wasn't for that, Lindy and Bernadette would still be alive. I believe the PAC must have planned it although I can't see what their reason was. I mean it was a multi-racial pub. The whole area is non-racial. OK I'm white but Bernie was coloured. The guys that pulled the triggers were pawns, they were brainwashed, they were filled with so much hatred, indoctrinated with hatred; they just did it because they were told to do it: the motive came from higher up. The others behind it are also guilty. But I don't think this government will take the matter any further after the trial. And yet if those guys are found guilty, I think the PAC should pay compensation. I need financial recompense because this has cost us a lot of money and is going to cost a lot of money for the rest of my life. I feel the PAC should pay for this.

I suppose my anger will lessen over time: you come to accept these things. But I don't think I will ever come to accept that I'm going to have to be in a wheelchair for the rest of my life. Even so I am not going to go out and shoot blacks. I never felt that way. The anger was about being a victim of a situation in the country of which I was innocent. I was an innocent victim of a situation that was not my fault, nor was it my fault that other people had such hatred in them. This is something I shall always be angry about. I think people who shoot others should just be aware of the absolute suffering and misery they are causing to the people they wound, to their families and to the families of those who are killed. I just wish they could feel what that is like.

Sometimes I think Lindy is in a better position, those are the times when I think about the pain I'm going through. And then I think about how lucky I am to be alive. Maybe it's contradictory to say these things; but I have been given a second chance and I've already come a long way. I can just hope for the best. I honestly think I could have died that night. I was given a second chance. If I'd lain there for ten minutes longer I would have given up. I would have just closed my eyes and given up. If I had relaxed mentally I would have died.

I am not very religious in the sense of church-going, but I have faith. I believe in God. I believe real justice will come one day when there is the judgement before God. This helps me. It does allow for a type of revenge.

Quentin Cornelius voted on the first day of the elections at an old-age home where the facilities were easily accessible to the frail and the handicapped. It was the first time he had cast a vote; he did so without any grand feelings: 'I obviously felt that I could not vote for any "black" party, as I felt that they were terrorists and murderers and I did not want people like this to be at the head of our country. But then the attack had taken place under a "white" government that was also unable to stop the violence. So I couldn't vote with full confidence for any specific party, but hoped for the best outcome. In the end it is a government of "unity" and not really a black or a white government. All I can hope for is that they bring justice to what happened, and that they find a solution to curb the violence for ever.'

Michael January is twenty-seven years old. In an unpublished letter to the *Cape Times* he wrote:

Much has been made of people affected by violence around the country — and quite justifiably too, but not much mention has been made of the many people who have been killed, maimed and crippled in various acts of terrorism in this country. These victims are in almost all cases ordinary people who happened to be in the wrong place at the wrong time. I obviously cannot speak for all such people, but I feel that we are being left out in the cold.

During the time we talked I asked him if the attack had changed his vote. 'No,' he said. 'I stuck to my political ideals. I voted ANC. I wore their badges. The attack probably made the act of voting more poignant. I felt it wasn't just an empty gesture: it was as if the fate of the country rested on my individual vote. It was a tremendous feeling. Once I had cast my vote I felt so wonderful.'

This is his story:

I was hit just below the left hip. I have a hollow stainless-steel pin permanently inserted inside the remnants of my thigh-bone. The pin extends from my hip to my knee. I have lost virtually all sensation in my lower left leg as a result of nerve damage, and have no muscle control in that part of my leg. A nerve-graft operation will hopefully restore feeling and movement to my leg and eventually I shall be able to walk again.

My parents are pensioners; my father has a car and he takes me to the physiotherapy sessions three time a week. The costs of my medical treatment come out of his pension. My DTP business had been running for three years but I had to close it down in January because I could no longer supply the service and I had to sell my computer equipment to pay for my operation and hospital expenses. I am now totally dependent on my parents.

On the night it happened my cousin and I had stopped at the Heidelberg to have a beer before going home. I think the last time I went to the Heidelberg was at least five years ago. We had just sat down when the attack started. I had heard shooting before but I didn't realize what was happening, I thought it was a gang fight out in the street, but I threw myself down anyway. I couldn't see anything because I had a table in front of me but I realized they were shooting into the place and that it was a terrorist attack. I tried to keep absolutely still. The shooting stopped after a few seconds; I heard people starting to move around, and then they began shooting again. I was looking in the direction of the door but I couldn't see anything except the window in the front of the place. There must have been someone shooting from outside because I could actually see holes appearing in the windowpanes. I remember thinking, Why doesn't the window burst? Shortly after that I was hit. I then expected to see someone walk past in front of me and put a gun in my face and shoot me. I was expecting to be hit in the face and chest. I put my hand to the wound and I could feel it was about as big as my palm. Blood was coming out between my fingers and running like water on the ground. I could hear over the noise of the shooting the sound of running water except it was my blood running out.

I have no idea how long the attack took, it seemed to take a long time, but it probably wasn't. It just seemed to go on and on and on. It probably lasted for at least a full minute and I wouldn't be surprised if it was even two minutes. At the time all I wanted to do was get out of the place and go home. I was worried about what my parents would think of my wound and how I was going to hide it from them. It was a bit like being a child again and not wanting anyone to know you had been hurt.

When the shooting stopped, my cousin asked me if I was OK and I asked him the same question then I said I was hit in the leg. He told me there was a grenade lying on the floor. I told him to get outside quickly but he said he couldn't leave me. Then a man who said he was a doctor took off his T-shirt and balled it up and stuffed it into the hole in my leg. People were stacking benches around the grenade. By this time I was just letting things happen. I knew the grenade was there but I didn't worry about it.

You see, when the shooting started I felt convinced I was going to die. I said to myself, Michael, this is how you're going to die. All I could do was lie there and wait for it to happen and wonder if it was going to hurt. I still can't believe that I didn't die that night. I remember thinking, Michael, you desperately want to black out now and wake up when it's all over. My teeth were chattering, my skin was tingling, my face felt as if it was being drawn in and I desperately wanted to be unconscious. I have a policeman to thank for keeping me conscious. He started asking me for my name and address and age and insisted that I answer him and that's what kept me conscious. He kept me talking all the time and once I had a hold of myself I didn't want to black out any more.

In the days afterwards I didn't want to have anything to do with anyone. I knew people had come to see me but I couldn't be bothered to speak to them. I hardly had anything to eat or drink. People told me to snap out of it, that I couldn't go on like that, but I wasn't interested. I just gave cursory comments to whoever wanted to speak to me. Then on the Monday a week after the event I made a decision to make an effort to speak to people. By the Friday I realized there was nothing more they could do for me in hospital so I insisted on being discharged and went home.

What I cannot understand about the event is why I was singled out to be a victim. Why was I singled out by a particular group as if I was responsible for the misery they were feeling, and therefore it was OK to shoot me? I know the whole thing was random but I feel I have been particularly victimized by the PAC.

I often think about the attack if I haven't got anything else to keep me busy. It affects everything, everything you think about. When you lie at night you are uncomfortable. It took about four months before I had the strength to move the blankets with my left leg. The weight of the blankets on my leg kept me awake. I would lie on my back and remember that was how I lay when I was shot and then I would think of the gunmen and think they were getting away with it. There are PAC people sitting in Parliament earning big salaries, laughing up their sleeves. To them it's absolutely nothing. I wish I could sue them for a million, three million, five million. Although actually the money is not important to me. I just want to feel that in some way I have got back at them. Yes, I want revenge. I want recognition on their part of what they have done. Of what myself and others are going through. I can tell you that I wonder at night about shooting a few people in the leg. And at times like that I think I am justified in doing it. They shot me in the leg and they are getting away with it: why can't I do likewise to them? To tell you the truth, I don't think so much about the actual guys who did it. As far as I am concerned if they are sentenced to life imprisonment or death it doesn't matter to me. But what about the leadership of the PAC? What about people like Patricia de Lille, who now sits in Parliament, what does she think? To me the leadership is responsible in principle. What anger I feel is directed at the PAC; but the government also seems unwilling to do anything about helping or recompensing victims like myself. I have lost a whole year out of my life and it will be another two years before I have the use of my foot back. I don't know how I'm going to cope with the rest of my life: this is going to be me alone against the world. I'm not going to get any assistance from anybody.

To be honest about it, the event had a great deal of religious significance for me. I wouldn't go so far as to say I had a premonition about it but my parents and family will tell you that on Christmas Eve I made a point of telling them what a wonderful life I had had, and that I believed God was looking over me. I felt that something wonderful was about to happen. I was convinced that my life was over and I had had a wonderful life. Four days later I was shot. When I was shot I was convinced that this is what I had been building up to, and this was how I was going to die. In some sense I feel God chose me to experience this and I feel I have now been given a mission. You could say I have been given a second chance.

The last person I saw was Ginn Fourie. We sat in her sitting room in the late afternoon and the light turned grey in that room and seemed to stay gloomy all the time we talked. There were long silences as she recounted events. She kept apologizing for being emotional. I thought that, like Quentin Cornelius and Michael January, she had an exceptional courage. At the end of the interview she talked about God. She thought that he looked on human affairs with a great sadness.

This is what she told:

We didn't hear about Lindy's death until the next afternoon. We had spent the day with friends in the winelands and we hadn't seen newspapers or heard the news on the radio. But when we got home friends were sitting in their cars outside our house, waiting. As we pulled up, one of them, Ray, came towards me with a card and a rose and because I hadn't seen him over Christmas I thought this was a belated Christmas gift. But I could also see he wasn't looking happy. Then one of the others, Dee, said, 'Sit down, I want to tell you something.'

I said, 'Don't mess with me, what's happened? It's Lindy isn't it, she's dead!' When they told me what had happened I said, 'I don't think I can cope with this.' We came upstairs and phoned the mortuary and they told us we could come and identify the body because at that stage there was no confirmation that it was Lindy. Before we left we even phoned her flat but of course there was no reply.

There are no words to describe the shock and grief I went through until the funeral: a numbness and inability to focus on anything but Lindy's death. There were things to be done and I did them mechanically. With the funeral the healing finally began.

We had a holiday in June and I thought that maybe it would be hard because I hadn't dealt sufficiently with the grief. I had been working on a thesis during December and I carried on writing, maybe because it was one way of coping with Lindy's death. But when the holiday came I was a bit worried that maybe I had allowed the work to stop me coming to terms with the grief. But actually the holiday was a good one. We talked about Lindy a lot and that helped. I have such wonderful memories of her. And I am at peace with her death. I have actually forgiven the men who did it. In fact I telephoned the criminal investigator and asked if I could see the men to tell them I had forgiven them. But the authorities wouldn't allow it. However this is something I will pursue. Of course I want to see justice done but if it is not done, and in this country and in the world it has not been done so many times, why should I insist that it gets done? It was hatred that led to Lindy's death. My thesis is dedicated to her and I refer to her as being a victim of hatred in our land, as so many others have been. I believe the only way we will counter hatred is by absorbing it and not hating in return. If those men are given amnesty, I would like them to know that I have forgiven them.

I don't think my life will be dramatically changed because of what has happened. I can't really say that I feel hurt, except by the silence of the politicians, and the government of the day. We never received any personal acknowledgement of our loss. There will just be an immense gap and a sadness. I miss and will always miss Lindy but I feel that she's safe from any further problems.

As for this country I think we may be able to absorb some of the hate. I still feel optimistic. Perhaps the elections were not the joyful occasion for me that they would have been and were for others, but I am still confident about the future. I have faith, if anything that has been strengthened. The prayer I prayed at Lindy's funeral has been reinforced over the months.

The last part of Ginn Fourie's prayer reads:

> My heart is broken
> The hole is bottomless
> it will not end
> But you know all about it
>
> Thank you for the
> arms,
> the lips,
> the heartbeats
> of family and friends to carry us.
>
> I trust you with my precious Lindy
> I know that you will come soon and fetch us
> O God
> I wish it were today
> But I will wait for your time.

Apart from the profound grief and suffering, there is common to the accounts of Quentin Cornelius, Michael

January and Ginn Fourie a disappointment with those who govern. It must be shared by the relatives of Simon Nkompone and Teboho Makhuza and Theo More, and by the mother and father of eleven-year-old Patrick Gasemane, the victims of the AWB killers. And it must recur bitterly in the thoughts of Petrus and Abrahm Mothupi and William Segotsane, who like Cornelius and January will remain physically scarred. These are the names I know: the list of the wounded and bereaved can be extended by hundreds of thousands. I do not imagine they will ever be compensated financially, nor will their pain be acknowledged by a note of compassion from those in power, or from those who were in power. This is indicative as much of official indifference as of how power was (and may still be) understood here. The state was supreme: the lives of its citizens could be callously sacrificed.

Just why this attitude prevailed not only has to do with the years of apartheid but with an inheritance that is much older.

8

The PAC has a slogan: 'One settler, one bullet.' It is, admittedly, not much heard any more but it was heard throughout 1993 and early 1994. In its simplicity it tries to write on to modern-day South Africa the story of nineteenth-century colonialism. In this story the settlers describe the natives as savage beasts; and the natives describe the settlers as pale ghosts without any compassion or humanity. In this story violence liberates both the colonized and the colonizer: it justifies the colonized taking their guns to blow away the colonizers. 'When the peasant takes a gun in his hands, the old myths grow dim and the prohibitions are one by one forgotten,' is the way Jean-Paul Sartre put it in his preface to Frantz Fanon's *The Wretched of the Earth*.

> The rebel's weapon is the proof of his humanity. For in the first days of the revolt you must kill: to shoot down a European is to kill two birds with one stone, to destroy an oppressor and the man he oppresses at the same time: there remain a dead man, and a free man; the survivor, for the first time, feels a *national* soil under his foot.

And as Fanon writes so graphically later in the book: 'For the native, life can only spring up again out of the rotting corpse of the settler.' In other words, for Fanon this is the only way the colonized can once again take control of their history.

Perhaps it was something like this that motivated those who perpetrated the Heidelberg pub massacre. At least within this ideology the deaths of Lindy-Anne Fourie and Bernadette Langford and Joe Cerqueira and Rolande Palm are not murders at all but part of the 'cement' which is mixed with 'blood and anger' to build up the nation, to use Fanon's metaphors. Ironically this is true. But it is not true in the way he meant it, because its logic also applies to the AWB atrocity. Those who commit massacres, irrespective of their political intentions, are killers, and they will remain for ever condemned by their actions. Neither they nor anyone else is liberated (or protected) by the bloodshed. They will never be heroes; they will always be murderers.

But what they did, those men of both the AWB and the PAC, was write two more incidents into history which, even though they emphasized the opposites in society, created a common past. This, I suppose, is the paradox of history: that although it is so often a record of human misfortune this misfortune is what identifies a people. It is the story of how we live. It is what defines us. Out of these traumas, historiography has it, the future is made; even such uplifting moments as those on 27 April. Again: perhaps because of such violence people found it in themselves to 'do good' as they did over the days of voting. But whether it is this good or that evil, both are written into history and both describe us. Nothing that can be called freedom grows out of Fanon's rotting corpses: over time the flesh perishes to leave dry skeletons, the bleached bones that we cannot ignore, and this may be called history.

These bleached bones tell us about the past. And some of the past, particularly the previous centuries, can be seen in terms of the colonial conflict Fanon describes. When the Heidelberg pub massacre occurred, I was exploring a small packet of family documents relating to the Eighth Frontier War between the Xhosa and the settlers, fought in the Eastern Cape from 1850 to 1853. In a way the Heidelberg attack became yet another vicious detail of that vicious war. Read as part of the frontier turmoil, it was a wholly consistent event in that war and for a moment I thought history had cracked and the Maleficents had stepped into my present. These were the people my forebear William Gray had fought for the possession of land. And they were still fighting (although their actions seemed pointless given that there was now a negotiated constitution, an election date, every indication of a political transition), and William Gray was dead, killed in a minor skirmish on 1 June 1851. Colonialism did not die with him, but in a metaphysical sense it ended as far as I was concerned. The details of his death (in one respect the 'blood' and the 'cement' Fanon talks about) became for me the words with which I could start to construct a narrative of living in South Africa.

Once, in my twenties and early thirties, I had felt marginalized, written out of history, or, more perniciously, not a part of history at all. I had left the colony created by apartheid but there appeared to be nowhere else to go. I drifted into a type of exile, a homelessness, the no man's land of the expatriate. Others I knew, who also felt this way, changed their geography, went back to England or to other 'settler' countries. But that did not seem an answer either. I believed that would only exacerbate the situation.

Life without history obsessed my early work: it supplied the stuff of lyric poetry, verse that is neither narrative nor dramatic but suited to the quiet personal statements of the lost. However, there came a time in the early Eighties when the poetry no longer seemed good enough: a weak cry of woe was not a gesture. Clearly it was destined for silence and the silence was preferable to continued lament. My attentions shifted to prose, where the words increasingly demanded a sense of the past. Slowly I began to discover the waiting country and with this my obsessions changed. I realized it was too easy to feel marginalized. There was a past with all the elements of colonialism that had to be recounted. I felt if there was any kind of beginning to the story it was here, and it became important to know how someone like William Gray had responded to his age.

In the months before the elections this task became ever more pressing. I did not see it as a catharsis or an atonement. Guilt was not the motivation: I did this because I was curious and because I was compelled by a need to record what was unacknowledged in my family. We were not the passive people I had thought. Once again the narrative changed, as I found that we had bled and that we had caused others to bleed.

Also among the family papers was a medal, evidence of what it had been like for my grandfather to live here. He, I began to realize, had taken part in what can only be seen as acts of repeated slaughter. I was horrified at the events he had been a part of because in their way they foreshadowed the AWB roadblock. Yet he and William Gray had behaved the way their times demanded and from that perspective they did no more than what was expected of them. They behaved like settlers. They took up arms against the natives to kill or be killed. I can see no sense in condemning them now. There are fundamental differences between the political conditions of their time and those of today. For one thing the settlers are no longer settlers. For another the armed struggle was officially over some time ago. However, what they did is eternally present, as T. S. Eliot pointed out, and, more importantly, unredeemable. Which provides an imperative to recount their stories.

The Eighth Frontier War was not only the second-longest war in South African history but also, in terms of the numbers killed, the bloodiest war between black people and white people fought on the continent in the nineteenth century. It was the most merciless of the frontier wars and gave rise to atrocities that repeat and repeat for us.

The historian J. B. Peires offered some explanation for this outbreak of vindictiveness in his book *The Dead Will Arise*. He put it down, in part, to *iqungu*, the supernatural forces which Xhosa warriors believed were generated in a soldier's stomach during conflict. This *iqungu* rose from the dead to destroy the killers unless it was dissipated through the mutilation of the corpse. Consequently, whenever they could, the Xhosa ripped open the stomachs of their dead enemies. In addition, certain parts of the body, such as the liver and the skull, had magical properties which were useful in the preparation of potions to ward off harm. The acquisition of these parts caused further violations of the slain, until, Peires observes, 'The sight of their dead comrades, usually disembowelled and sometimes decapitated, roused the British soldiers to a pitch of fury.' And then a reciprocal bestiality was unleashed.

The pitch of this fury can be found in the matter-of-fact prose of one Stephen Lakeman who, for his own pleasure, formed a militia to fight in the war. He records being asked by a doctor to 'procure for him a few native skulls of both sexes', a task which his men 'easily accomplished'. What they did next is best told in his own words:

One morning they brought back to camp about two dozen heads of various ages. As these were not supposed to be in a presentable state for the doctor's acceptance, the next night they turned my vat into a cauldron for the removal of superfluous flesh. And there these men sat, gravely smoking their pipes during the live-long night, and stirring round and round the heads in that seething boiler, as though they were cooking black-apple dumplings.

The skulls, it seems, fetched a good price in the universities of Europe.

It was in this climate of maliciousness that William Gray, a field cornet responsible for military matters in the Southwell district not far from Grahamstown in the Eastern Cape, rode out one bright winter morning to his death.

Gray, apparently, was a much respected man. He had sailed to South Africa from England at the age of nineteen on one of the first ships to carry what were to become known as the 1820 settlers. Despite the hostility along the eastern frontier, and the intermittent wars which drove him from his farm and even saw the farmhouse burned to the ground in 1834, he prospered as a sheep farmer. His obituary records that he married Elizabeth Marsden in 1830; that he was a member of the Lower Albany Agricultural Society in 1845; that he entertained Sir Harry Smith, newly appointed Governor of the Cape, at his farmhouse in 1847; that he was a committee member of the Eastern Province Agricultural Society in 1849; and that his appointment as a field cornet was made in 1850. From the family papers I learned that he had three sons and four daughters and 'was a very happy man, always singing songs to his children'. From R. Godlonton, the editor of the *Graham's Town Journal*, I read that 'Field Cornet Gray was amongst the most enterprising of the first Albany settlers. His character was unimpeachable, and his loss [was] justly considered a calamity to the whole settlement.' And in Commandant Thomas Stubbs's *Reminiscences* was this description of his family's grief: 'I never wish to see another sight like the one I saw there on arrival. Mrs Gray and her children rushed into the wagon where her dead husband lay. Their cries were something terrible.' His gravestone, wrongly dated, in the small cemetery at Southwell is inscribed: SACRED TO THE MEMORY OF WILLIAM GRAY, LATE FIELD CORNET OF SOUTHWELL WHO WAS KILLED IN ACTION NEAR THE KARRAA BY THE REBEL HOTTENTOTS OF THEOPOLIS 2 JUNE 1851. AGED 49. It says that his death is 'sincerely regretted' by his family and his countrymen. Beneath that is the inscription THE LORD KILLETH AND MAKETH ALIVE; HE BRINGETH DOWN TO THE GRAVE AND BRINGETH UP.

Southwell cemetery was a good place to sit on a clear July day with the poinsettias red along the wall and the empty trees combing a warm dry wind in a constant sibilancy. A chest-high stone wall covered in lichens and moss separated the graves from dense bush on one side, and from the mown lawns that surrounded the stone chapel and the long, whitewashed manse on the others. There was no one about.

I first entered the chapel where bats chirped in the rafters and their droppings littered the flagstone floor. Behind the altar was a stained-glass window dedicated to the glory of God and the memory of William Gray. Small brass plaques on the walls told of the lives and deaths of other settlers. Two unlit candles stood in their wax on a marble shelf that had been presented to the parish by the Dean of St Paul's, London, after the cathedral was partly destroyed by bombs on the nights of 9 and 10 October 1940.

I went back to the graveyard and sat on the tombstone. I thought of the remains of William Gray beneath me: the skeleton that would be matted into the clothes he had been buried in. And I thought of the two lead balls, misshapen by the impact with his body, which had ended his life and lay now among his bones. And I wondered what he had thought when the first had ripped into his stomach. What was in his mind as he lay waiting to be helped away by his comrades? Did he think he was going to die? I had with me a copy of a letter written to one of William Gray's daughters by the Reverend Henry Tempest Waters, who seemed to think he may have been prepared for death. Two paragraphs read: 'Several rebel men were seen to fall, and on our side we suffered having six men wounded: but worst of all your dear father was called away from the miseries of this sinful world. He died fighting a righteous cause, and, I have reason to hope, was prepared for death.'

When I left I placed a stone for him on the grave. I had spent almost two hours in the solitude. It was one of the most peaceful places I had ever visited.

I do not think William Gray died for a righteous cause. He died because it is always easier to settle disputes with bullets than it is to settle them with words. It seems that a group of Khoikhoi living at Theopolis Mission, which was run by the London Missionary Society, grew restive at their conditions and rebelled. The first William Gray knew of this was when a Fingo, loyal to the settlers and 'almost in a state of nudity', arrived on his farm, which was less than ten kilometres from the mission, with the words, 'Master, we are all killed.' The man then described how

On waking this morning, I saw a party of Hottentots stationed at the door of each of the Fingo huts, and as the Fingoes attempted to come out they were shot. I saw my father and brother and a man named Zwartboy fall, and then ran for my life. I believe they have killed their own Hottentot headman. The work of death was going on when I made my escape. Several volleys were fired.

153

By now Gray could hear the shooting. He could probably also see smoke as what was then the oldest mission station on the frontier burned. He rode to Grahamstown to get help and returned the following day with the Albany Rangers led by Thomas Stubbs.

Stubbs fulfils the archetype of the tough frontiersman. He responded to his age decisively, quickly and violently. In his book *Frontiers*, Noel Mostert tells how Stubbs specialized in a war tactic described as 'waylaying'. He and his men would conceal themselves on either side of a footpath and wait patiently and silently from dark to daybreak until a group of Xhosa came down the path. They would then shoot them mercilessly. I do not know if William Gray took part in such ambushes, but, of course, the probability must be admitted. Stubbs professed repugnance for his scheme but it was obviously not strong enough to make him desist.

'You hear them coming on,' he wrote, 'perhaps humming a tune.'

You see them and almost look in their eyes and you have to give the signal for their death warrant. I have heard people talk very lightly about shooting Caffers, but I believe it is by those who have never experienced it. But I have always felt grieved that my duty compelled me to it. You certainly don't think much about it after the first shot is fired. But before that, and after the excitement is over is the time any man must feel it.

The British officers thought it both 'unsoldierlike and un-Englishmanlike to waylay', but Stubbs informed them that his idea was 'to destroy all the enemy without being killed myself or losing my men and shall continue that plan as long as I have anything to do with the war'.

This then was the man who hurried the Albany Rangers along the grass flats reaching from Grahamstown to Theopolis. They would have skirted black kloofs that cut into the flats and are thickly wooded. Giant euphorbias rise from the bush in these ravines and among them stand aloes red-headed at this time of year, their broad leaves extending out like arms, coarse, studded with thorns. Over this terrain William Gray would have passed towards his death.

This is Stubbs's laconic account of the skirmish:

We had about two miles to charge and just as we turned the corner of a small hill we came upon them . . . The firing was kept up for about two hours when I saw J. Woest being carried out by some Dutchmen. He had received a bullet through his knee. Shortly after E. Dell came to me with his hand to his side and said he had got one in his body. I gave him some gin and water to drink and examined his wound and found the bullet had struck him just below the ribs but had turned out again leaving a wound about four inches long. When he found there was nothing serious, he threw his hat up with a 'Hooray' and started back, as he said, to have another go in. W. Gray, Field Cornet was next. He received a shot in the stomach and was being carried out by two men when he received another wound which killed him.

Which killed him.

They are quick simple words and they raise no senti-mentality. This is what happened to settlers on the frontier 150 years ago. That it is still happening to farmers in the region says something about the inefficacy of bullets to settle disputes. But what intrigues me about the words is how they fastened William Gray into history. The story of his life is greater than the life he led, if only because it will last longer. And now I have become his author. His story is my story: I can tell it to suit my purposes; to show how, like a word in a sentence, I have my place.

The death of William Gray has symbolic weight. I find in it a moment of epiphany: the nature of being here. There is contained in this perception the violence of the past and the violence that occurs now and that which is still to come. In the middle of the Eighth Frontier War a missionary declared in despair: 'Any way you turn . . . in South Africa, there is blood.' Yet he continued. The truth of his words remains with us. Yet we continue. This reality brings out a stoicism. I have no regret at what might have been, nor is there a purpose in speculation. Whatever footfalls echo in the memory are those that lead down a path that was taken. This acceptance engenders a hope. And even if the hope exists only in that moment when the surface glitters, it is enough.

I try and remember this when I think of the stories my grandfather told me. I must admit they contain elements that make me uneasy. Not only because of what happened but also because they force me to wonder if in the same circumstances I would commit similar actions. Actions which must rightly be termed atrocities. I do not know how I would react. I believe such responses are part of what it is to be human. This does not give me much hope that I would behave decently.

What my grandfather did and witnessed must have been buried deep in his life. And yet I remember a man who held my baby sister as if she was delicate porcelain. There is no contradiction here: the capacity for violence does not exclude compassion in an individual. Those who committed murder in the Heidelberg Tavern or on that Western Transvaal road will be known by others for the love they gave. Maybe one day (if they do not hang) they too will tell grandchildren of the deaths and suffering they unleashed in the world. I remember my grandfather as a man who was kind to me, who gave me sweets and, more significantly, gave me money to buy sweets. There are photographs of him playing with us, his grandchildren. He is always smiling. I remember there were soft dewlaps of flesh beneath his chin and so much skin on his face that it seemed to be folded into layers like neat laundry.

He created for me an enchanted world of high adventure. It was a place of outlaws, pirates and renegades, of Blackbeard and Rob Roy and Dick Turpin and of wild days on the frontier fighting Zulus. A world without history. A world of make-believe, except it was some time before I started to separate the fantasy from what had happened. That both were told within the same vocabulary kept the essence of the events that had occurred obscure: figures floating in never-never land. But as I got older some images softened and disappeared while others hardened and would not go away. By then it was too late. I could not go to him for further explanations. He was dead. And, as with all legacies, I had to reveal it on my own.

For two decades his stories have risen periodically within me. They would ache like gallstones and then dissolve, only to return a few years later. I kept on refusing to meet them, continuing to believe they belonged only to the enchanted world. And then I came across the medal and a photograph. There was an insistence in these artefacts I could no longer ignore.

The photograph shows my grandfather upon his horse. He is nineteen, dressed in the uniform of the Umvoti Mounted Rifles with calf-length leather boots. He sits easily upon the horse, looking down along his left shoulder towards the photographer, and there is something in his face and the tilt of his head that is familiar, that I recognize as my own. It is disconcerting, this, as if in a way I am him and what he told me are my memories, not the residue of second-hand stories. His expression is serious, his lips are firmly closed, his gaze distracted. He is not armed. In fact there is something paradoxical about the photograph: the background tangle of aloes and bush, the domesticity and the patience of the horse, set against the earnest formality of the rider in a high-buttoned jacket. Here is a young man who helps his father in their butchery in the back settler country responding to the call to restore law and order because two white men have been killed and white-owned pigs and white-feathered fowls are being mysteriously and symbolically slaughtered on the farms and smallholdings. On the back of the photograph is pencilled his name: Wallace Alkins Westbrook; and the place: Sterkspruit Hotel, New Hanover. The names are an amalgam of European colonial history.

The medal is now pinned to the bookcase beside my desk. The ribbon is a deep crimson edged in black. It is threaded into a clasp dated 1906 in raised numerals. On the medal itself is depicted the female figure of Natalia trampling on a Zulu shield and assegais: she has a large sword in her right hand, a palm-frond in the left. Behind her is the helmeted figure of Britannia holding a tasselled standard and the orb of peace. In the middle distance gather a group of subdued Zulu men. It is dawn: the sun rising through dispersing stormclouds. On the obverse is the uncrowned head of King Edward VII with the imperial inscription: REX IMPERATOR. Some ten thousand of these medals were awarded, with royal approval, to those who served in what was then called 'the Natal Native Rebellion of 1906'.

In April of that year my grandfather answered 'the call to

arms', as he would have phrased it, and was mustered into the UMR. For the next three months he and his comrades would kill men, sack kraals, burn crops, confiscate cattle, arrest and frequently flog anyone suspected of rebel tendencies. Before this ruthlessness, Zulu dissidents fled to the Nkandla Forest where they gathered under Chief Bambatha. Yet their guerrilla campaign was desultory and disorganized. They were kept on the run by the colonial militia (which was made up of hundreds of well-armed men) and when they were engaged in skirmishes their casualties were high. In Mome Gorge some five hundred were killed in a morning; in the Umvoti valley a similar number died as the troops 'drove' the rugged kloofs and densely bushed terrain. These 'engagements' and others like them were not battles, they were routs. To the colonial forces they were regarded as 'mopping-up operations', yet even the Governor of Natal and a senior official in the Colonial Office used the words 'continued slaughter' and 'massacre' to describe the suppression of the Zulu impis, who were armed, mostly, with assegais. During the winter months some three thousand Zulus were killed, seven thousand were imprisoned and thirty thousand were rendered homeless. How many were wounded is unrecorded. We do know however that, in the rage to punish, some seven hundred Zulu men were flogged so badly their backs were 'lashed to ribbons', to quote the contemporary writer Captain James Stuart, and that more than five thousand sentences of flogging were carried out. Against this it must be recorded that eighteen white soldiers died and six civilians were killed.

My grandfather told nothing of this. He left the history for me to read up. His stories were selective: they were merely the key to unlock the box of my inheritance.

As I recall it, he told me these brief accounts one summer

afternoon in my middle teens. He lay propped up on his bed in his grey flannels and his white open-necked shirt. His feet were in slippers, his ankles a flash of white, an almost luminous white, between them and the turn-ups of his trousers. The radio was tuned to a cricket match but the players had gone in to tea and the commentators were analysing the slow overs that had just been played when I brought him his tea and biscuits. He was rubbing the carved knob of his walking stick at the gap between his eyebrows. The flesh there was always pink. From the distance came the happy screams of children playing at a neighbour's swimming pool and the drone of a lawn-mower.

He waved his walking stick to indicate I should sit down on the edge of the bed.

I did so, curling a leg beneath me. He started to speak.

'Did I ever tell you about . . .'

Maybe this piece of his past had come suddenly to him that afternoon and he felt the need to tell it. I can imagine the details repeated in his life on such quiet moments, with the force of them gripping him in their endless time. Maybe then he was frightened. Maybe then he pushed the walking stick hard against his forehead, seeking to wipe them out.

I have a feeling he chuckled as he told the first story and warned me never to drink from a stream unless I was at its source. Of the second revelation he made no comment that I can recall. Of the third he said the Zulus did it as a warning to all whites. He said it was a horrible sight: that it raised a fear in him and his comrades, but it also made them angry.

What he told me was how they found a dead Zulu lying bloated in a spruit after they had watered downstream. He said some of the men retched at the sight and one of them shot the corpse. He told me that they hanged three men. And lastly he told me of a flayed man whose mutilated corpse was meant to warn all whites of the fate awaiting them.

These are the stories he left me. I cannot get rid of them. I can imagine the shooting of the corpse. I can see the three hanged men. I realize he must also have witnessed or been part of the execution and corporal punishment of scores of men. The UMR was one of the regiments chastised by a magistrate for its unjust floggings. My grandfather was not at Mome Gorge but he was part of the force that 'drove' the Umvoti valley. And here, I think, is where the flayed man, one Oliver Edward Veal, comes in. Veal's butchered body was found by the troops near a deserted kraal. His body parts had been hacked away to be used as 'medicine' in what James Stuart calls the process of 'doctoring for war'. Stuart also notes that the skin had been cut away from the soles of Veal's feet but that was as far as the flaying went. However, it was enough to convince the soldiers they were fighting demons and may have led to 'the ferocity of their subsequent actions', as the historian Shula Marks puts it.

I cannot pretend the details about the militia's behaviour do not affect me. They are deeply disturbing. But I would rather know them. I would rather know how we have lived here. Essentially, they do not alter my memories of the man: he is remembered still for his kindness and the fantasy world he gave me. Yet I have had to add the ability of savageness to him I called Grandpa. I have to believe he was capable of killing. But, more exactly, I have to realize he killed. This is not a trait usually associated with grandfathers. Yet there is a way in which I accept it. I understand that for him this is what it meant to live here. So I accommodate these excesses in the stereotyped image of a grandfather if only because my own responses to war (or the type of 'war' he fought) are, thankfully, untested. I turn as well to W. H. Auden's poem 'Spain' for a way to deal with this legacy. It makes sense to say that history, and those of us who inherit it, 'may say Alas but cannot help or pardon'. It is a harsh morality, but one well suited to harsh times. In this scheme my grandfather's story is part of history but I can also choose, and have chosen, to make it part of now. Which is why I have told it, as I told about William Gray, because all we have to treat the past is simply the telling. And if we fail here, I think something in us may be lost.

9

There is also this about the events William Gray and my grandfather were involved in that I find unnerving: others died, and they have disappeared. It is likely that the warriors of the Bambatha rebellion still live in an oral tradition, but what of the Khoi fighters who were killed in that skirmish on 1 June 1851? I do not think there will be any oral tradition to preserve them.

The settler Thomas Stubbs recorded that 'several had been shot and many more died from wounds'. In his statement there may be a degree of colonial exaggeration, to aggrandize their efforts that day, but it is likely some Khoi did die. They will have no stone tablets honouring their lives, or stained-glass windows dedicated to their memories. They are anonymous in history. I could not find out who they were or where they were buried. Their bones probably lie in the kloof, unmarked. History has not named them because history is usurped by those who write and who build and who leave behind traces of their existence. History also belongs to those in power who control the reproduction of 'true events'. What happened or what may have happened becomes of less concern than what should have happened. The narrative is arranged to reflect the glory of the writers. But there are bones on the veld that have worked their way to the surface: they have to be written back into history. Especially now they have to be acknowledged.

The importance of this occurred to me at Lidice, a small village thirty kilometres outside Prague that was razed by the Nazis in 1942. It was an act of vengeance because the Czech resistance had assassinated General Heydrich in Prague. Like all acts of revenge it was simple and brutal. The men were massacred; the women and children loaded into cattle trucks destined for the concentration camps. Then the village was fired.

When the war ended, the survivors of the camps returned to rebuild their village, but this time on top of the hill. The site of the old village they planted with roses. A small memorial museum stands alongside. The curator is one of the few remaining witnesses. Inside against a wall are passport-size photographs of all the men who were killed. Against another, photographs of all the women who succumbed in the camps. I was fascinated by the photographs: the confident faces, the pride, the simple expectancy that life would not betray them. We have all had such photographs taken. Yet who, staring at the camera, could imagine this horror? That one day they would be machine-gunned to death. That one day they would be herded like cattle to places of incarceration. That this innocent photograph would become their memorial.

A video compiled from original film footage taken by the Nazis showed the German occupation of Prague. Soldiers goose-stepping down Wenceslas Square past statues I had marvelled at just the previous day; gun-carriages being drawn across the Charles Bridge where I had walked despite the biting cold. And then the grotesque scenes of the massacre, the departure of the women and children, the destruction of the village. When it was

finished I wanted to get outside, away from the claus-
trophobia of the small viewing room. The curator opened
the door and nodded with a smile. I went out into a snow
that was thickening in the air and beginning to settle.

But at least there was a memorial, I thought. At least no
one could forget.

The same cannot be said for two small groups of people
who suffered similar fates in 1921 and 1922. What
happened to these people settled so relentlessly in my
imagination that it became the basis for a novel, *This Day
and Age*. But it was not until long after the book was
finished that I went to pay some kind of homage at the
sites. Mostly, the violence done to these people has been
lost in the vastness of the South African veld. But perhaps
now, as we begin to re-create ourselves, we will reclaim
them.

The event of 1921 concerned a religious sect known as the
Israelites. What I remember most about the place of their
slaughter was the heat and the dust and the flies. Even at
eight o'clock in the morning the heat was powerful and
blasting. I remember the gravel road came over a rise and
went gradually into a long flat valley. We stopped there to
consult the map and watched the heat shimmering above
the scrub. Karoo koppies rose in front: flat-topped hard
hills of ironstone and whitethorn. This was Bulhoek. It was
here that on 24 May 1921 – Empire Day and the birthday of
Prime Minister Jan Smuts – a force of more than eight
hundred policemen and soldiers opened fire with Maxim
guns and rifles and in twenty minutes slaughtered 183
people and wounded one hundred more. It is not an incident
that gets much space in South African history books, if it is
mentioned at all. But it has deep roots within the community and has created a hero of mythic proportions.

The previous night Jill and I had spent at a camping park in the nearby dorp of Queenstown. The attendant there told us an apocryphal story of a man who had hopped on one leg, because his other had been shot off at the knee, from Bulhoek to Queenstown. He had staggered over a harsh terrain of thornbush and gullies and scattered rocks. He had hopped all afternoon and all through the night to cover the thirty-odd kilometres. The attendant said it was a miracle the man had survived. He also said that although he himself was not an Israelite he believed their leader, Enoch Mgijima, was a true hero of the people. Every year, he said, in all the churches in Queenstown, except for the Afrikaans Dutch Reformed church, memorial services were held for those who had died at Bulhoek. He said the spirit lived on.

This was in my mind as we approached across the valley. The road curved down towards a drift that crossed the Swartkei River, the banks rising steeply and eroded on either side.

In Robert Edgar's booklet on the Israelites, *Because They Chose the Plan of God*, there is a photograph of the troops crossing at this drift on the day before the massacre. It shows a team of six horses pulling an artillery piece up the embankment. Leading the horses are three mounted soldiers, bandoleers of cartridges slung over their chests, their faces shadowed beneath pith helmets. Behind them come more mounted troops and in the distance, entering the sharp decline to the river, is a small truck. The veld looks brittle and dry: I imagine it yellowed by the start of winter. Probably the river was no longer flowing but had become a series of stagnant pools.

We went, as the troops would have gone, into the drift. There had been some summer rains and the river ran thinly across the causeway, yet was still little more than a stream linking the pools. In one a woman washed clothes but did not look up as we drove across. The soldiers would have come up on the far side and seen against the koppies the village called Ntabelanga – 'the mountain of the rising sun'. It was not there any longer. Sparse veldgrass and stunted whitethorn trees covered the ground where the village had been. For afterwards it was razed: the thatched roofs torched, the mud walls destroyed with axes. Yet even now there were vague rectangles in the earth where the houses had stood, a ghost image forcing history to remember.

Down the road came three children: two girls dressed in white frocks and a boy in a white suit holding his shoes in his hands. At the massacre the people had been wearing white tunics, which had made them easy and obvious targets for the soldiers. And all because white had a special meaning. There is a verse in Revelation which goes:

> And when he had opened the fifth seal, I saw under the altar the souls of them that were slain for the word of God, and for the testimony which they held: And they cried with a loud voice, saying, How long, Oh Lord, holy and true, dost thou not judge and avenge our blood on them that dwell on the earth? And white robes were given unto every one of them; and it was said unto them, that they should rest yet for a little season, until their fellowservants also and their brethren, that should be killed as they were, should be fulfilled.

We looked around and noticed other people going to church, moving like white spectres through the scrub. The children came up. They wore blue ties, the flat knot carefully positioned in the centre of their chests. Pinned on each was a cardboard medallion bearing a photograph of their prophet, Enoch Mgijima. He stared out implacably, his eyes narrowed and the skin pouched below them, his lips set harshly beneath a patchy moustache; a demeanour almost of disdain. He was a man regarded now, even as he was then, with awe.

The children were latter-day Israelites. Followers of a man who, in the first two decades of the century, had preached his millennial visions and offered a temporal and a heavenly freedom to people who had been dispossessed of their land by the 1913 Natives Land Act, ravaged by disease during the 1918 Spanish-flu epidemic, seen their livestock diminished by droughts and were being hounded about the countryside by frightened white farmers who threatened to shoot them on sight.

It was little wonder that a man who spoke for God, prophesying the day of judgement and retribution, should attract ever more adherents. Especially as he had also established a community that did not pay taxes, proclaimed Ntabelanga 'holy ground' and had charged his lieutenants to be uncompromising in their dealings with white officialdom. Little wonder, too, that his sect created consternation among whites and their government. A fear that was brutally expressed in *The Star* of 17 May 1921 by someone who signed himself Night Bomber:

> When dealing with natives and especially with the religious fanatics like the 'Israelites', enough stress cannot be laid upon the value of moral effect. These natives are looking for martyrdom. Why not save white men's lives and natives as well with as little bloodshed as possible. Half a dozen low-flying aeroplanes, using a few bombs or machine-guns, would clear up the trouble quickly, safely and cheaply — besides creating a lasting impression on the rebel mind. An aerial strike would never be forgotten.

There was a belief among the Israelites that in a

confrontation with the authorities five months before the massacre, Enoch Mgijima had turned their bullets to water. Certainly the police had fled, leaving their food and equipment behind them, a humiliation which the government found particularly galling, especially as the Israelites were armed only with knobkerries. And the words of a policeman who admitted that 'when we pulled the triggers we found the bullets had turned to water' had become part of the mythology.

From the few photographs there are of Enoch Mgijima it is not difficult to feel the compulsion of such stories. In one, he stands in full ceremonial robes looking down at the cameraman. His face is resolutely composed; his right hand clenched over the knob of a waist-high stave; his left hand holding a bugle. This is a man who may well have shouted, 'Jehovah says you must charge the Heathen' – and sent his followers into the relentless bullets.

I asked the children if we were on the road to the mass grave. The elder girl pointed farther down the track. We drove on across the ground the Israelites had charged over in their brave and useless attempt to defend their own. Few had reached the police lines. Only one policeman was slightly injured, for the Israelites had no weapons other than knobkerries and assegais.

We came to the grave. It was surrounded by a high fence fringed with barbed wire, yet the gate was not locked but held fast by a strand of wire. Such protection seemed incongruous in this hidden valley. We went in.

The grave was rectangular, raised three bricks high, the retaining wall newly whitewashed. There is a photograph, probably taken on the afternoon after the massacre, of the bodies lying in this shallow grave. The width is that of two men, laid length-out. This is hard earth in which to dig a grave: baked stony ground. In the photograph a soldier stands looking over the corpses; on the veld behind them are gathered some Israelite men.

The grave, like the memory of those needlessly dead, was well tended. On the tombstone at either end were inscribed biblical references. One from the Psalms was: THEY HAVE TAKEN CRAFTY COUNSEL AGAINST THY PEOPLE, AND CONSULTED AGAINST THY HIDDEN ONES. THEY HAVE SAID, COME, AND LET US CUT THEM OFF FROM BEING A NATION; THAT THE NAME OF ISRAEL MAY BE NO MORE IN REMEMBRANCE. FOR THEY HAVE CONSULTED TOGETHER WITH ONE CONSENT: THEY ARE CONFEDERATE AGAINST THEE. The end of this quotation pleads with God to take revenge on the tyrants, to PERSECUTE THEM WITH THY TEMPEST, AND MAKE THEM AFRAID WITH THY STORM. Beneath the references were the words: BECAUSE THEY CHOSE THE PLAN OF GOD, THE WORLD DID NOT HAVE A PLACE FOR THEM.

The government had regarded the Israelites as squatters and ordered them to move off. Jan Smuts, as Prime Minister and Minister of Native Affairs, had refused to intervene although they had asked to see him and promised to abide by his decision. Christian missionaries looked askance at Enoch Mgijima's teachings. Most whites and even some black leaders called the Israelites 'primitives' and 'fanatics'. In a parliamentary debate on the massacre John X. Merriman said: 'Anybody who studied it saw that it was a very dangerous thing indeed. The idea was ... Africa for the Africans, that Africans must combine and sweep the white man out of the country.' And later, when Enoch Mgijima was brought to trial and sentenced to six years with hard labour, the judge said that the Israelite leaders had used 'their religion as a cloak' to propagate the 'crazy notion that the day was coming when the black man would have his freedom'.

We left the grave, fastened the gate. The heat was solid now, the flies insistent. A herd of goats moved languidly among the thorn trees. We drove off. In their church, a small white building, ramshackle beneath a corrugated-iron roof, the Israelites were singing.

Apart from the two mass graves there is no official memorial to commemorate the Israelite tragedy. Nor are there signposts to direct those who may wish to stand at the graves and remember.

A year later, in June 1922, a similar act of suppression occurred in the dry fastnesses of the northern Cape and southern Namibia. At the time Namibia was known as South West Africa and was administered by Jan Smuts's government. On this occasion the authorities took the advice of the anonymous 'Night Bomber' and sent, along with the regiments, their cannons and their machine guns, two aeroplanes. The tactic was recommended in a contemporary editorial in *The Cape Argus* for having a 'chastening influence on the disorderly elements among the native community'.

In the winter of 1993 Jill and I drove across hundreds of kilometres of dust and desert to try and find the place where the Bondelswart had been massacred. My purpose was really just to stand in the still veld that would no longer bear markings of the tragedy and try to imagine the sheer human terror. The roar of the planes coming in low and loud, the explosions, the cattle running berserk, people screaming, and from the koppies the steady rattle of rifle-fire. I wanted no more than that: an hour imagining. Somehow it seemed important that what was a mere paragraph in history be reimagined in its intensity. As if in telling it again we could learn something more about ourselves.

So I had gone to Warmbad, which had once been the Bondelswart capital but was now a forgotten, crumbling village with a hot spa that attracted no one. It was here I thought the massacre had occurred. And it was here, beneath a picture of president Sam Nujoma sticky-taped to the corrugated-iron walls of a classroom, that I met the grandson of the legendary guerrilla leader Abram Morris.

I had gone to the school to ask for information about the rebellion but the headmaster had not heard of the battle.

'Wait a minute,' he had said and left me staring at Nujoma. When he returned he was with a short, sharp-faced man in a tweed jacket.

'*Ek is Meneer T. Morris*,' the man said as he introduced himself.

'Morris!' I repeated in surprise. 'Any relation to . . .'

'Ja,' he said, anticipating my question, 'the grandson of Abram Morris.'

I had not gone looking for Morris. But when I heard his name I could not believe my luck.

We walked outside, where I explained my intentions. I showed him all I had by way of historical reference, a now much folded and grubby photostat of a short entry in *An Illustrated History of South Africa*:

> In June 1922 the Smuts government . . . came under severe censure for its expedition against the Bondelswart tribe of South West Africa who had become restless as a result of objections to escalating taxes demanded for keeping their hunting dogs, and complaints about white occupation of land. The government force lost two men; 115 Bondelswart men were killed in action and women and children were killed and wounded by bombs.

'It didn't happen here,' was Morris's first response. 'It happened at Haib.'

I took out a map and spread it on the bonnet of the car,

weighting it down with a Roberts *Birds of Southern Africa* and a pair of binoculars.

Morris started talking about his grandfather.

'There wasn't anyone who could shoot a rifle better than him,' he said. '*Ek se vir jou hy was goed.* He was damned good. He'd fought the Germans in 1906, killed them like flies in the gorges of the Orange and Fish Rivers. The authorities feared him. He was on the side of the South Africans in the First World War: they knew what he could do. On that afternoon, when the planes came over Haib and he saw them dropping their bombs on the women and children and machine-gunning them while they fled, then he aimed at the pilots and killed one. The plane crashed in the veld next to the village and the wreckage lay there until 1964 when the South Africans came and took it away. And you know why they took it away? Because over the years, you see, they became ashamed of what they'd done. They didn't want to leave any sign of what had happened there.

'But there are still the graves of the women and children they killed. And the hurt is still here in our hearts. The people still cry about that time.'

He looked at me sharply: 'There are things that are not in the history books or in the report of the commission of inquiry but I have got documents to prove they happened. You give me your address. I shall send copies.'

Then he stabbed a finger at the map.

'You go there, to Haib,' he said. 'You ask for Jakob Swartbooi. He'll tell you about it. He'll show you where the plane crashed.'

I thanked him for the information he had given me and for that still to come.

'Just tell Jakob you saw me in Warmbad this morning,' he called out as we drove away. 'He'll tell you everything.'

Quite unashamedly, Meneer T. Morris was lying.

Admittedly only about one small detail, but it was an instructive lie none the less. While we stood in the rough schoolyard at Warmbad hugging ourselves against the cold Namibian wind he looked up at me without a hint of unease and told his wishful story about his grandfather. And at the time, and for days afterwards, I believed him. More significantly I wanted this to be the way it had happened: I wanted to believe him. After all, it was now a commonplace in war reports to have planes shot out of the sky in balls of flames and black smoke. So why should not his grandfather have turned his rifle-fire on the two planes that were causing such devastation among his people and livestock, and brought one down?

In a way fictions of this sort even up the odds a little; serve to remind that a desperate people with their Mausers and Enfields and black-powder muskets once rose against the state because it was the only alternative left them. And no matter how hopeless their puny weapons they felt they had a moral right which could not be gainsaid, which they thought would be enough to bring them justice. Surely Morris's story had the details of history and the power of myth. It deserved to be true.

It was an hour's drive to Haib, along the empty gravel road up from Warmbad to Karasburg then west to the few scattered shacks at Haib in what is still called the Bondelswart Reserve. On the way I wondered about Morris's notion of the South African sense of shame: shame had never been overly noticeable before in the state's handling of unrest. But it did not seem an entirely fanciful idea that a rusting aeroplane engine could become a symbol of an atrocity that was considered best covered up and forgotten.

At the time I knew nothing more about the Bondelswart rebellion than the information on the photostat. It was only later, encased in the black shell of a microfilm unit in the

174

South African Library, that I realized a story of ruthless suppression and a blind madness to exercise power lay behind the bland history. Slowly it revealed itself as I scrolled on and on through the dense type of the contemporary newspaper reports, searching for Abram Morris's humiliating rifle-shot. I could not find it, but I did learn that this was the first time South African aeroplanes had been used against local citizens.

In other documents I read of Colonel Pierre van Ryneveld, commander of the Air Force detachment, and pilot Lieutenant John Daniel inspecting on foot the aftermath of the bombing. About them the commandos set fire to the Bondelswart huts and smashed wagons in a frenzy of destruction. Horses burned, and from every side came a wail of human tragedy and the yowls of mutilated cattle. Through the smoke and noise a woman dressed in bloody sheepskins approached the two airmen and told that her child had been blown from her back. Van Ryneveld moved on, muttering: 'Gunners' work, not mine. That's gunners' work.'

Perhaps this story, recounted by Daniel to writer James Ambrose Brown when he was researching the rebellion for his 1971 novel *The Return*, shows something of the shame Meneer T. Morris was talking about. But if it does then it was barely a whisper, soon deafened by reports of the mistreatment of prisoners and the remorseless way in which Abram Morris and his men were tracked down.

Despite the horror of the aerial attack on Haib, or maybe because of it, Abram Morris did not consider surrender. Instead, that night he and his men slipped away, hoping to find refuge in the canyons of the Fish River and in the kloofs of the Dead Mountains. But it was not to be. The next day the aeroplanes spotted them and they were harried and pursued into the gorges of the Orange River.

There a few days later the 'firebirds', as they had become known, surprised them at dawn. Forty twenty-pound bombs were dropped and some two thousand rounds fired from the machine guns as the aeroplanes strafed the valley.

At first there were reports that Morris had died in this attack, but his last stand was to be made two days later on 4 June at a place called Berg Kamer, where he and fifty-three of his men died.

But all this information I was only to come across much later. Now we saw the shacks of Haib approaching and turned off the gravel road on to a track that led to a group of tin shanties where some people stood warming themselves in the mid-morning sun. I stopped the car, got out, approached them. They watched me without any sign of welcome. I asked for Jakob Swartbooi and was told he was not there. Then I explained about Meneer T. Morris and said I wished to see the graves of those women and children who had died during the bombing. And perhaps there was someone still alive who had witnessed the attack?

They consulted among themselves and the one who had elected himself spokesman told me there was one person, Aunty.

'Do you know about the rebellion?' I asked.

They smiled and shifted about, seeming coy and embarrassed.

'We have heard there was a war,' the spokesman said.

'Do you know about an aeroplane that was shot down here?'

They looked vague. We stood in awkward silence for a moment then I asked for directions to the graves and to Aunty. The spokesman, Julian, said he would come with me. As we turned to leave, a man touched me on the arm.

'I'm Jakob Swartbooi,' he said. He wore a balaclava, which he now rolled up to expose his smiling face.

'Why didn't you say so earlier?' I responded.

'I thought you were police.'

We both laughed nervously.

'Can you tell me about the aeroplane that was shot down here?'

He shrugged his shoulders and turned away: 'It was far out there in the veld,' he said, waving vaguely towards the south. And that was the end of it: he would not be drawn further.

'Julian will take you to the graves,' he said. 'You go with him.' He smiled again. 'I can't help you. I have to go to Karasburg.'

I made room in the car for Julian and we drove down the donkey-cart tracks to Aunty's. Julian was twenty. He had finished school but he did not have a job and not much prospect of one either. I asked what he was going to do. He did not know. Then in my question I heard a historic echo. It was because the Bondelswart lived off the land, and did not need to do anything that could be defined in the colonial mind as 'work', that the 1922 dog tax was imposed to force them to find employment on surrounding white farms.

Had he heard anything about the rebellion from his parents, I wanted to know, still believing that somewhere an oral tradition kept the event alive.

No, he said. Once he had asked but his mother had grown angry at his questions, saying that it had nothing to do with him. So he had left it. We drove the rest of the way to Aunty's shack in silence. It seemed to me profoundly wrong that what had happened should fade out of memory.

Aunty was wizen and bent and crackled with life and good humour. She must have been in her eighties. She told how she had been surprised by the soldiers while she was drawing water from the river on the morning of the massacre. She had fled back to the village. She could remember in the afternoon a plane flying low over the village and how she and her mother and sisters had taken shelter in a cave on one of the koppies behind the village. She had heard the bombing but not seen it. They had stayed in the cave all night. And the next morning she recalled there were soldiers everywhere and much confusion.

I enquired about the destroyed aeroplane wreckage but she knew nothing of that. Then as we said goodbye she asked: 'En Master, wat is Master se ras?'

The question flustered me. She wanted to know what race I belonged to. Her words carried a lifetime of servility and a history of racism and they seemed so completely out of context. I think she meant was I British or American or Australian, because she was surprised by my answer, as if it was not the obvious one at all.

'South African,' I replied.

'So,' she said, nodding, frowning, her face for a moment serious.

Then she seemed to recover and laughed and waved as we drove off.

The graves of the nine were scattered over a small area in the scrub beyond the river. They were unmarked heaps of stone. I tried to imagine the shattered and torn bodies that had been buried here, but the images remained elusive. Had they been buried where they fell? Was one of them the baby that had been blasted from the woman's back? I walked among them. Not a whisper came off the stones and the scrub, not a trace of what had been done.

That night at a guesthouse in Port Nolloth I met Matthew, the resident amateur historian. I asked him about the bombing of the Bondelswart.

'Flour,' he said. 'Bags of flour dropped to scare them. Remember, it was 1922, aeroplanes weren't fitted to carry bombs. Anyhow, just the sight of an aeroplane would have been enough to put the fear of God into them. Oh no, they weren't bombed by anything but bags of flour.'

I thought of Meneer T. Morris's story of shame. Here was an adjunct to it, another story based in shame. Perhaps there really was a conspiracy to hide the truth. But no matter how much I wanted to believe Morris's story, in the end I could not. Was it honestly likely that the Nationalist government, at the height of its apartheid powers, would have felt the slightest remorse for actions committed forty-two years earlier by Jan Smuts? It was decidedly unlikely. No, Morris's story was a fascinating bit of myth-making, a desperate longing to try and redress the imbalance of power. Nowhere could I find mention of a downed aircraft. Not in the contemporary newspaper reports, not in the report of the commission of inquiry, not in the history books nor in any secret military documents that might have been hidden in files these last seventy-odd years. Perhaps Meneer T. Morris created his story because he did not expect me to go to Haib or check the details. Who knows? Needless to say I did not hear from him again.

There are some who say that the telling of such events should be left to the people themselves; that in the retelling one is again usurping history. But those who say this still see history as the separate stories of separate groups of people, and I do not believe they are right. In a fundamental way we all belong in the narrative. Like Meneer T. Morris, some of us, those of us who are concerned about such things, are reimagining the narrative because history is as much an expression of emotion as an expression of facts. And so I have told these stories partly to explain what I called earlier our 'context of violence'. Repressive actions like the campaigns against the Israelites and Bondelswart, and the viciousness with which the Bambatha rebellion was suppressed, have bred into successive governments an indifference towards individuals and communities. And this indifference, which at its most extreme places no value on human lives, has permeated throughout society. It can be seen in the AWB and PAC slayings; it can be seen in the daily acts of violence.

I have also told these accounts because 'the need to know what has happened' has become a compulsion in these cold days. This need has been specifically focused on the apartheid years, where the memories are closer and still raw. But we should not forget the deeper history too. It seems important that, unlike Julian and his friends, who admit to little knowledge about the attack on their forebears, we do not find ourselves in the same position.

10

The need-to-know expressed itself early in the weeks of grace that attended the election and the inauguration and the opening of Parliament. Although the mood in the first weeks of winter was determined by a small stock of reconciliatory phrases that we used to talk about ourselves and the country, there was inserted into them a notion that the past would not easily be erased. At first this idea was vague and ill-defined but it soon came to take on a more serious purpose.

So although we referred to 'our beloved country' and our 'beautiful land' and of 'black and white together' and of the 'rainbow people', and the need for 'absolution and reconciliation' to allow for a 'healing process' that would lead to the 'building of a nation', the words began to acquire an edge. People were saying 'forgive and forget', but then these people tended to belong to the *ancien régime*. They sighed with relief when the new president appeared to espouse this magnanimity with his 'Let us forget the past. What is past is past' speech. He too felt that it was time for the 'healing of wounds' and the building of bridges over 'chasms that divide[d] us'. But the clichés and the abundance of metaphors veiled another intention.

There were some early indications of just what this

intention was when Mandela opened Parliament in mid-May. He now talked about how 'the burden of the past' lay 'heavily on all of us, including those responsible for inflicting injury and those who suffered'. Thus there was a need to prepare 'legislation which [would] seek to free the wrongdoers from fear of retribution and black-mail, while acknowledging the injury of those who [had] been harmed so that the individuals [were] identified and attended to'. In their offices the police and Army generals must have been given pause by these words and wondered quite what they meant.

About this time Judge Richard Goldstone, who for the past three years had headed an inquiry into political crimes, was awarded an honorary degree by the University of Natal and in his acceptance speech he talked about a 'compelling temptation to forget the past' because it avoided 'painful confrontations, trials, lies, fear and even violence'. He said this was unacceptable, that it was a 'recipe for national discontent' and would probably lead to past abuses being repeated. He felt that what was needed was an exposure of past crimes. And that the way to do this was through an official Act of Parliament. He referred to the 'astounding manner in which black South Africans appeared to forgive' and 'the apparent absence of hate and of a desire for revenge'. Despite this he said there was 'deep, deep hurt and pain in the hearts of many' and that an 'official exposure of what caused their hurt and suffer-ing' was the only way to enable them to 'begin their healing'.

I wondered if Judge Goldstone had been thinking of Vaclev Havel's comment that those who could not be truthful about the past would not be truthful about the present. Or more particularly: 'Whoever fears to look his own past in the face must necessarily fear what is to come.'

Either way, the judge was laying the ground for what was to become a much contested subject.

It was not long after this that Dullah Omar, the Minister of Justice, began to talk about a Truth Commission, an idea that seemed Orwellian but, we were told, had worked successfully in Chile. There, a commission had investigated political killings and disappearances during the military rule – not to prosecute those responsible but to establish who should be compensated for the state's violence. To qualify for indemnity, those who had perpetrated human-rights violations would have to tell the commission what they had done and to whom. Those who were not prepared to do so and were found out would be prosecuted. Omar stressed that the South African version would not lead to 'Nuremberg trials'. Rather it was a chance for the victims to speak, because, he said, no one had a moral right to forgive on their behalf. In the middle of June he told Tim Modise on Radio Metro, 'I believe the truth is good for our country. I want to make a break with the past through a commission of truth and reconciliation,' as the proposed commission had now been named. A week later a radio reporter quoted him saying, 'This government must be seen to be different from the government of the past. We must make a break from the past, it is the only way of healing the wrongs. We must create a society in which people respect one another as human beings.'

Predictably, not everyone agreed with Dullah Omar. The *Weekly Mail & Guardian* pointed out that a truth commission could become a way of 'managing and controlling and ultimately hindering' the business of exposing apartheid crimes. The editors warned darkly of those who over the decades had become practised in creating judicial diversions that had rendered so many commissions of inquiry impotent. If this was going to happen again, they said, then rather leave the task of investigation to journalists.

At an economic forum in Cape Town, Deputy President de Klerk told delegates a truth commission would undermine the good will and sense of national unity which had 'taken root'. He then changed the metaphor to make use of the medical terminology that was so freely being borrowed to diagnose the moment, and said a truth commission would tear 'out the stitches from wounds which are only now beginning to heal'.

Over the weeks the rhetoric became increasingly heated and recourse was made to philosophers and political scientists to bolster the arguments. From the University of Cape Town, Professor Hermann Giliomee quoted Alexis de Tocqueville's dictum that 'one is apt to perish in politics from too much memory'. He felt that unless the commission commanded respect across the political spectrum its chances of establishing the truth and fostering reconciliation were 'remote'. Giliomee's concern was that, instead of restoring respect for the rule of law, a commission of 'hand-picked politically correct judges' would merely form a separate system of justice. He envisaged what he called 'spooks from the netherworld' coming to confess their crimes and also to implicate their superiors, who in turn would lay bare the chain of command, right up to people sitting in the cabinet of the government of national unity. The political costs of this, he warned, would outweigh any moral gains. And, as if to emphasize the point, one of the generals let it be known that a truth commission was not only an 'exercise in futility' but would mean that leading ANC cabinet members would be required to appear before such a commission and that they would be severely embarrassed by the information the police had on them. This general was none other than the Commissioner of

Police, Johan van der Merwe. Among the figures he named were Deputy President Thabo Mbeki, Defence Minister Joe Modise, Housing Minister Joe Slovo and PWV premier Tokyo Sexwale.

At issue here were probably the concentration camps the ANC had used, as they put it, to 'discipline' their cadres during what are rather grandly termed 'the years of armed struggle'. These camps had been the subject of an internal inquiry by the organization and although a report had been released no disciplinary action was ever taken. This despite evidence of victimization, torture and deaths. And, bizarrely, of shopping raids into South Africa to buy expensive shoes and clothes for Modise, then an Umkhonto we Sizwe commander. In response to the general's threats it was soon being said that nothing the ANC had done could be compared with the evils of apartheid, and that ANC officials would be more than prepared to give evidence. The major crime, people were saying, was state violence conducted by the police, the security police and whatever other covert operatives were employed.

By way of an example of the sort of abuses being discussed here, the newspaper *South* ran this story:

A few years ago an MK soldier was arrested by security police. During the arrest, police shot him. He was treated in hospital, then taken to a police cell. There the torture started.

A pipe in his leg to drain out fluid from the gunshot wound was yanked out by a security cop. He was repeatedly beaten on the open wound with a police baton.

He was left to lie in the freezing cold. Medication was denied him. At one point, knowing that he was deeply religious, a cop proceeded to sodomize him and make him perform fellatio. When the cop finished sodomizing him, he brought in common law criminals and in turn they raped the MK soldier while cops cheered.

That was not the only torture the soldier endured while held under Section 29 of the Internal Security Act.

Today the soldier is free and relatively successful. One of the security policemen is dead but the one [who was] in charge is still on the force.

The policeman was not compelled to do what he did in carrying out the duties demanded by the apartheid government. He did not have to resort to barbarism.

At the end of the article the MK soldier commented: 'I will never never forgive them. The only time I will be at peace and accept the changes in the country is when they punish those bastards for what they did to me.'

There is something about this story that rings untrue. Perhaps because the original incident has been so drastically summarized and perhaps because there is almost an obsessional concentration on the various rapes, the tone seems wrong, too sensationalist. But the point is that, although the content may not be true in any strict sense, it carries in its essence a type of story that has been too frequently told to be dismissed.

It struck me when I read the piece, and it still feels apposite, that we need a truth commission; but I do not believe this should lead to forgetting nor, for that matter, to forgiving. For many people, once there has been confession and sincere contrition, forgiveness would be a natural and humane gesture. I am not so sure. Forgiveness may be too easy, a way of dispensing with a horror which really cannot be buried. Although whatever was done was done at an extraordinary time, the time of apartheid, this does not essentially offer any excuse for what now is regarded as barbaric behaviour. Perhaps we should remember that barbaric behaviour is not aberrant at all: it is what people will do given the opportunity. For this forgiveness is inappropriate. 'I am not inclined to forgive,' Primo Levi wrote of his Auschwitz persecutors, 'because I know no human act that can erase a crime.'

Nor should refusing to forgive be confused with seeking revenge. Revenge is too simplistic and tends to encourage further violence. Rather, being unforgiving means the guilty have to admit culpability and acknowledge a darkness that cannot be eradicated and is with us always. They become symbolic of the darkness; their names become the mirror image of our own. They are there to tell us that we are all capable of betraying our humanity and that forgetting this cannot be countenanced.

The point was made poignantly for me in Elisabeth Reichart's harrowing story *February Shadows*. Her book is based on a historic incident: the hunting of five hundred prisoners who broke out of the Mauthausen concentration camp in Austria on 2 February 1945. Seventeen survived the frenzied chase to recapture them. The rest were murdered by the National Socialists and the inhabitants of the nearby villages, who up to that night had been 'non-political'. Reichart's novella tells of the painful remembering of Hilde who, as a child, witnessed this atrocity and then for the remainder of her life sought to forget it. But the trying to forget ruined her, destroyed her relationships with those she loved, both husband and daughter, brought in the shadows of the title. Finally, years later, her daughter forces out the memory and the horror, the guilt, the shame is revealed in short bitter sentences. The revelation is too late for Hilde; she has been poisoned by the process of forgetting. Quite what this means in psychological terms for an individual is, Reichart shows, a loss of compassion. Early in the story Hilde remarks that the only way to survive is to forget: and yet to do this she has to dehumanize her world completely. She does not use a possessive pronoun to refer to 'her' mother or 'her' father but calls them 'the mother' and 'the father', emphasizing her alienation from them. She refers to the emptiness she feels after forgetting and describes it as a 'feeling of becoming cold'. 'Maybe', she reasons, 'death had begun with some people in this manner. That they became cold.' And that memories of them become cold as these people pass out of mind. Forgetting, as Reichart points out, is the beginning of our death. Easing that death is the apparent charity of forgiveness.

Some years ago when the war started in Bosnia I remember reading of an eighteen-year-old girl who became an expert torturer. It was said that before the violence started she was a responsible, intelligent scholar, much admired by her friends and her elders. Had the war not begun she might never have known the cruelty of which she was so easily capable. Yet it had been latent through-out her eighteen years and probably, should she live to see peaceful times, will become latent again. Latent but always available. I do not believe she can ask forgiveness from those she wronged and if she did I do not think it should be granted. Forgiveness allows what is evil in us to recur just as it hides what has been done.

It is, I suppose, a kind of amnesia. We believe that once there is forgiveness a horror can start to be forgotten or at the very least the matter can be put aside, as if without this finality continuing would be impossible. So a torturer confesses and the victims absolve him. He, the torturer, humbled yet now pardoned, made virtuous again, goes back into his life a new man. And he, the victim, or she, the survivor of the victim, even if recompensed for his suffer-ing, for her heartache, could be forgiven for thinking that this is not enough, that again a wrong has been committed.

I think particularly here of Nyameka Goniwe, whose husband, Matthew Goniwe, was killed by a hit-squad. It may help her to know who did it and why, but it will not help us if those people are forgiven. In the vocabulary of the politicians, no wounds will be 'healed', no chasms 'bridged', no nation 'built'. To forgive is merely to use 'leaves and flowers' to cover the 'friendless bodies of unburied men'. The imagery is from the Elizabethan play *The White Devil*. As a metaphor it does not end there: it goes on to remind that the wolf remains at large and one day his nails will dig up the bodies. It is better, I think, to admit that the wolf is constantly with us, even when it cannot be seen and is inactive. It is better never to cease accusing.

Envoi

In August a malaise set in. People spoke of fatigue. They spoke of a weariness. A recurring flu rattled in their throats and streamed from their eyes. Their doctors prescribed tonics and rest but people needed more than medicine and time off. We all needed more than that. Things seemed to be out of control, sliding in all directions, and we, we were too weak to do anything more than lament. 'I just can't stand it,' my neighbour cried one morning. 'What's happening is too horrible.' Because the new story seemed so much like the old story and we did not know how to read it except in the old way.

'Life', Slavenka Drakulić wrote about the end of the Communist era in Prague, Budapest, Bucharest, 'has the same wearying immobility; it is something to be endured, not enjoyed.' She could have been discussing South Africa. There was a feeling that we were stuck, that we were continuing to repeat gestures without realizing their sameness.

There were strikes; there were fights between the strikers and the scabs; there was public molestation; there was merchandise destroyed; there was merchandise looted. Company spokesmen said strikers were demonstrating a new militancy. Since the election, they said, the workers had grown increasingly restive. At a supermarket, demonstrators poured methylated spirits on the floor and threatened to torch the building. Elsewhere, strikers attacked a convoy of vehicles with sticks and stones until guards opened fire and a man was shot dead. Elsewhere, managers were kidnapped and held in store rooms.

This was not a 'winter of discord', said Sam Shilowa, Cosatu's general secretary, on television, although many of us believed it was. He wore a white dove of peace badge on his suit lapel and smiled as he answered questions. Sitting beside him was Labour Minister Tito Mboweni, who said industrial action was normal for this time of year. In the newspaper the following day David Brink of Business South Africa was reported as saying his organization was not unduly concerned about the strikes. Yet the catering union was on strike. So were the dockworkers. The court interpreters were picketing at courthouses across the country. The automobile union was out. The social workers' union was out. In hospital canteens health workers *toyi-toyi*ed and discarded their uniforms in protest. In Natal nurses were on strike and soon it was reported that four patients had died because of the action. Construction workers downed tools. Truckers blocked the highways. The musicians' union demonstrated outside the SABC. The steelworkers threatened action.

Ostensibly what the strikers wanted were higher wages. What they wanted was more than an inflationary increase to make up for what they saw as the years of deprivation under apartheid. But mostly they wanted to see if things had changed. 'Our workers are saying that no one declared a honeymoon with the government,' said Sam Shilowa. 'We are being asked by our own members if democracy will ever mean anything more than the right to vote every five years.' Mostly they were being told that this was exactly what democracy meant and that essentially nothing was different.

A friend, well-versed in the ways of industrial action, voiced the hard-line attitude of business. The effect of the strikes, she said, would be insidious, difficult to attribute to management's future decisions, but the cause of things for all that. They would lead, she implied, to attrition. Companies would stop offering educational bursaries and housing schemes; they would close down stores where the margins were small, people would lose jobs.

These messages began appearing in the narrative sooner rather than later. Late in July *The Star* was editorializing about a 'fading euphoria'. The leader writer saw 'hairline cracks' in the economic scenario and said the projected growth rate of 3.5% was being 'hastily revised in the wake of fears of a fiscal crash' due to the labour unrest. Unisa's Bureau of Market Research produced an even lower figure of 2.2%. And from the *New York Times* came the news that foreign investors were finding 'a host of reasons to stay away', but mostly the labour troubles were cited as an 'unnerving reminder to investors that workers [had] not bought the new government's message of restraint'. Why invest in a country where the labour force was 'costly, unskilled and militant', where there were trade barriers, exchange controls and little chance that the expectations of the impoverished majority would be met? Almost anywhere else, the *Times* piece was reported to say, from Mexico to Brazil and especially South-East Asia, those with money to invest could get a better deal. Cheaper labour, higher skills, greater company loyalty, better production figures.

Also, the newspapers were telling us, the 'hundred-day honeymoon' in Parliament was over and the politicians once again had their knives out. This, we were told, was how it should be in a democracy. We were told by political commentators that when the parties snapped at one another it kept everybody alert. But, I could not help wondering, what sort of democracy was this? Perhaps it was a democracy because there was universal franchise. Perhaps semantics kept us from being called a one-party state. Semantics and the fact of the government of national unity. Yet even here mutters were being heard that showed there was a crack in everything. Had not National Party leader de Klerk warned that his party's participation was not unconditional? We had not heard this before. We had not even thought to hear it.

'Tell me what is going to happen in this country,' I was asked by a French academic during President Mitterrand's pilgrimage to shake Mandela's hand. But before the enormity of her question I could only shrug and stutter and fall back on the three words that made sense: 'I don't know.' 'Are you going to be like the rest of Africa?' she persisted. 'Can you tell me why Mandela must be paid so much money? It's more than Major, almost as much as Clinton. You must realize we see this as signs of corruption to come. We look at this and at the violence and we do not think this will remain a land of miracles.'

Neither did I, but then I did not think it was a land of miracles. And corruption was nothing new. For decades it had been the cornerstone of the National Party government. Like many I thought Mandela was paid too much. I thought all politicians were paid too much. I thought the bureaucracy was out of hand, but these things did not concern me as much as the constant deaths that occurred behind the day-to-day story of our lives. The violence had not stopped. It went on remorselessly. It went on as if nothing had changed. Families were gunned down while they ate supper. Men, women and children were stabbed and strangled and hacked to death with axes. Policemen were killed on the job. They were killed as they walked to work. This killing of policemen reached such a level that Safety and Security Minister Sidney Mufamadi called it a 'national tragedy'. With much despair and even more impotence, he said, 'It is time the madness stopped. The attacks are on a scale unprecedented throughout the world.'

'Ours is a completely lawless society,' said police spokesman Craig Kotze.

'We thought things would get better in the new South Africa, but they are getting worse,' said Colonel Ruben Bloomberg. 'If you wear a police badge you are considered a legitimate target.'

Were there 'illegitimate targets', I wondered? Were the senseless, random killings 'legitimate' or 'illegitimate'? Since the elections our vocabulary had changed. We did not talk of 'political' murders any more, which in some way had been 'legitimate' because we had been in an undeclared, non-specific state of civil war. They were now acts of criminal violence. After the seven members of the Ngcobo family were gunned down while they ate supper, the police said there was no political motive and that they would catch the criminals soon. But they never did. Just as all the other apparently gratuitous slayings went unsolved. People said there was a 'third force' loose in the land. Hired guns who owed no allegiance to anyone. Maleficents intent on mayhem!

Yet for all this, people said they were still guardedly optimistic; nobody would admit to pessimism; but the qualifying adjectives were back, taking the brightness from our nouns. And people used the phrase 'at the end of the day' more frequently. They were trying to convince themselves and others that 'at the end of the day it will be all right'.

*

All August I drove restlessly across the country, revisiting graves and massacre sites and places where battles had been fought, but they were mute. There was nothing more to be learned. I stood on the veld and gazed at the koppies and kicked at the ironstone beneath my feet which raised a fine red dust but little else. Once again I stood on the edge of the Magaliesberg and above me some fifty vultures hung and drifted on the wind that broke invisibly against the cliff and pushed upwards. Their wings were huge; knitted along the sky. They looked down watching, waiting, but, while there was death elsewhere, there was no death here. In them was so much grace, so much sheer competence at reading the wind and rising thermals. One by one they went into the heights beyond my vision. Their going left a sense of loss; it carried no metaphorical significance.

In Johannesburg I saw the sky become inflamed, the way miners had described it a hundred years ago when the dust blew up and a redness filled the air and stung those caught on the streets. I saw this red storm lacerate the suburbs and was alarmed by its wilfulness and the way it shook through trees and gardens. It swirled across the car and filled the interior, leaving my eyes raw, a thin grit on the skin. After the dust came snow: flurries that did not settle but brought a blinding brilliance to the light. The weather seemed demoniac. Just as the city seemed demoniac: a place of paranoia and urban terror. On Radio 702 people phoned in to talk to Dr D about sin: a man told of his hatred for his mother, who he thought was 'evil incarnate'; another said he prayed to the Lord to deliver us from the 'clutches of evil' that held the land in its 'grip'. People phoned in to describe to talk-show host John Berks how they had been mugged on the streets, raped in their bedrooms, stabbed in their gardens, and seen those killed who were attacked by car hijackers. They complained to

DJ John Robbie about the bad service in restaurants, the sour faces of shop attendants, the indifferent attitude of bankers. I listened to it and felt the wolf's claws scratch at my skull.

Like everyone else in his neighbourhood, my friend Derek had signed a contract with an armed-response unit. Like everyone else he displayed their logo on his gate, warning that a break-in would be met with swift and remorseless action. Inside the house electric eyes watched the rooms and passageways during the hours they were absent and during the hours they slept. He explained to me that if it went off men with assault rifles would come hurtling over the perimeter walls and would shoot anything that moved. 'I had to sign an exclusion clause,' he said, 'indemnifying them against accidentally shooting me.'

I drove out of the city as soon as I could. I drove, and rediscovered the unsettling power and truth of clichés: for this *is* a beautiful land. I went through grasslands that stretched yellow and vast beneath the streaming light. In the morning this veld crackled with ice; in the late afternoon shadows came on it like wings across the sun. At the end of the desert I saw mountains rising pale, massive. From their snowed peaks blew a wind that cut through the scrub where goatherds moved with their animals. On these brown plains the white of the goats caught the sun in haphazard flashes as if from a heliograph. At a distance they were signals I could not read.

On the car stereo I played Leonard Cohen over and over again. He intoned in his harsh whispering voice about things sliding in all directions, about there being nothing left to measure any more, about the 'blizzard of the world' that had overturned 'the order of the soul'. He said he had seen the future and it was 'murder'.

I thought he was singing about what it was like to live here now. I thought he had been along the road I drove. Because there is this about him: he can stare unblinking into disorder. He looks and records what he sees and returns to report to us with beguiling melodies and seductive background voices overlaid by his bass incantations. And we must listen because we know there is a message here we cannot afford to miss. We listen to the sadness in the voice and understand it does not issue from a man who wallows in misery. It does not come from a pessimist. It is bleak; it is sometimes touched by despair but it is always sung out of a deep compassion. For Cohen is no Isaiah, no St John the Divine: he does not bring us glimpses of the apocalypse; rather he is describing how we live and the consequences of how we live. He realizes there is little sense in going beyond this. He appreciates that the most that can be done to retain some humanity in the noise and chaos at the end of the millennium is to report and describe. But, of course, it is the way this is done, today's subtext, that counts as well. Because Cohen is truly subversive. Through the arrangement of a tambourine, a drum, a violin and the sweetness of the backing voices, he can gently mock his words and gently mock those of us who hear them. Here is the edge, the ambiguity and the enigma. What he would call the 'Awful Truth' that 'isn't worth a dime'. And so in the beautiful elegy, 'Anthem', he sings of the repetition of history and how we continue to ignore the signs that could avert our suffering. Until, with a chorus backed by the Los Angeles Mass Choir, he offers a paradox that is painful:

> Ring the bells that still can ring
> Forget your perfect offering
> There is a crack in everything
> That's how the light gets in.

198

Which *is* how it happens. Which is how we have brief moments of grace even in the midst of violence. Which is how our election happened and allowed the 'goodness' that we spoke of to prevail. And in Cohen's sung chorus there is a consolation that cannot be found in the words alone. They need the music and the choir and his voice of rust to arrive at what one reviewer called a 'quotidian valour', or, put another way, our recurring, daily bravery.

It was Cohen playing on the car stereo as I drove to interview a grieving man who was filled with savage despair. It was Cohen singing about democracy as I drove that day through an unseasonal gale that built sand-drifts on the tarmac and covered the way in a shifting whiteness. It was Cohen singing the song that had been sung at the inauguration of President Bill Clinton that I was listening to when a youth (I think of him as a youth) picked up a stone and from his place in the thick bush beside the road watched my car approaching, and waited, and judged, and at the moment he thought was right threw the stone in a perfect arc at me. And Cohen sang about democracy:

> It's coming from the sorrow on the street
> the holy places where the races meet
> from the homicidal bitchin'
> that goes down in every kitchen
> to determine who will serve and who will eat.
> From the wells of disappointment
> where the women kneel to pray
> for the grace of God in the desert here
> and the desert far away:
> Democracy is coming to the USA.

I saw the stone as it fell towards the car: a quick black object, and instantly I knew what it was. It missed the front windscreen by a hand's breadth and banged against the passenger door. I smiled. I thought of the Maleficents, and smiled. Of course that stone might have carried death. If it had smashed through the windscreen I might have lost control of the car. I might have swerved into the oncoming traffic. But speculation is meaningless. The stone and the unseen youth belong to this story and, more importantly, to this moment in the story. I travelled that road another five times in the next three days and the incident was not repeated. It was random, it was gratuitous: it had as much purpose as any of the other acts of violence.

There is also in this lyric about democracy an element of 'quotidian valour'. Cohen understands what it is to carry on in the face of our social ineptitude and he sees in this continuing a resilience. Perhaps this resilience is hope; perhaps it is no more than stubbornness; but maybe that is enough. Enough to make us imagine other ways of living. In the last verse of 'Democracy' Cohen likens us to plastic 'garbage bags'; it's a lowly image but it is a tough one. And it displays a kind of truthfulness which right now makes sense.

The man I went to see on that day of the stone had lost this resilience. He was decaying. He no longer had the will or the imagination to conceive of a different life. Also he had lost all faith in life: he could not hold up the hope that Cohen calls a 'little wild bouquet'. He was so filled with anger that nothing existed beyond it. I had never seen such grief before. It was the sort of grief that wanted to annihilate all those who were not grieving.

This man had lost his daughter in a terrorist attack. She was dead and he said half his life had been taken away. And the half that was left him was so consumed with hatred that he valued no one and no thing any more. He made a naught with the index finger and thumb of his right hand and held it at me as he said this. 'Friend,' he said, with all the venom of the word 'enemy': 'Friend, this is what I think of people now.' He said he had no respect for the new government. He said that of all humanity he despised politicians and advertisers and reporters most. To him they were scum. He did not say it but I was clearly included among them. He said he had phoned my publishers in London to find out if I had misrepresented my intentions. He said telling his story would change nothing. No one would listen. No one would care. They would say, 'Oh, shame,' and that would diminish him further. He said that no one, least of all a writer, could understand his pain. He said his life was private and the memory of his daughter was private. He had a responsibility to keep this sacrosanct, he said. 'You have to make money, friend,' he said, 'so you write your book. I have told you how I feel.'

For weeks I was troubled by the after-image of his face. It was pale. A trim beard edged the line of his jaw and the sharpness of his chin and encircled his mouth. As the days passed, his lips became thinner, were drawn in a tight line of hate. When he opened his mouth the darkness behind his teeth was the darkness of death.

When I remember this mask, because this is what it has become, I realize what we have lost. Beneath our anguish and our hurt and our pain lie buried the rituals we need to change ourselves. Once we dreamed of the end of apartheid but we did not dream of what would come afterwards. And now we are adrift. Once we spoke in slogans and rhetoric and now our language is bereft of meaning. We all knew apartheid would end yet we were defenceless against it. Over the years its perniciousness sank into our lives. Now we have changed the political system but we cannot change our personalities. Our characters, as Slavenka Drakulić wrote of her compatriots who lived under Communist regimes, 'have so deeply incorporated a particular set of values, a way of thinking and of perceiving the world, that exorcising this way of being will take an unforeseeable length of time.' I fear she speaks for us, too. We search through history and see division instead of realizing that this is our story. We look at ourselves and see differences instead of similarities. We cannot imagine how we could live differently.

We are, in every sense, alone with our day. It can be used or it can be discarded: the option is ours. Despite all the international well-wishing – the loans, the aid, the guarantees, the pledges, the favourable interest rates – only we can imagine how we wish to live. We have behind us the process of historical change, the ritual of how we described the world: the choices and the decisions for the future are ours. As Auden showed in his poem 'Spain', the ability to change is impressive and nations brought to pivotal moments in their history can either build the 'Just City' or agree on a 'suicide pact'. Whichever is chosen, history will accept, because, for Auden and for us, history is necessity: it is, as the poem argues, the moving story of what people did and how they did it, of reinvention and continuity; in other words, of ritual: the ritual of people reimagining themselves as they abolish a world of 'fairies and giants' and install 'dynamos and turbines'. But sometimes the sense of ritual gets lost in the immediacy of today's 'makeshift consolations'. Sometimes it does not seem possible or important. Perhaps then we should take a lesson from elsewhere, from, say, the lives of whales.

What the whales have to tell us has everything to do with ritual and place. I think their lives demonstrate the complexity of living and the importance of where they live. For they bring to the seas and the coastlines and the bays the ritual of their history. Unlike us they are unaware of it;

unlike them we have demeaned what it is to live in this place.

Every September the whales return here to False Bay. And every September I take comfort in knowing they are back. Inexplicably they swim out of the ocean currents into the bay. I imagine how, in the darkness of the sea, their tails undulating with the power of their motion, they follow invisible routes that are mapped in their genes. I can see their coming: silent vast shapes, grinning unchallenged through the inkiness.

Suddenly False Bay changes. That vista of sea, flat and green in the off-shore wind, scuffed with cormorants and the hard white of the gannets, becomes the place of the whales. It is their refuge now. As they have done over the millennia, they have come back to reclaim it. Between these mountains they have mated and calved and suckled their young. Their bones lie on the sea floor and under the sands of the beaches. Their blood was spilled in this sea when men hunted them here. When they leap in celebration of their mating they are proclaiming and re-enacting a way of life that has been theirs through the aeons. These are ancient rituals, ancient rites.

They come here to conduct two essential activities: to mate; and to give birth. And both are acts with long-established traditions. It is this ritual that I relish. This mysterious return and this mysterious going away. Because I have come to realize that the empty bay, the bay without whales, is as important as when they are present. It is always a refuge. And for this reason it would not have the same value if it was a constant home to the whales. Instead its significance lies in their return: that they have chosen this place, much as we choose places to build shrines or temples, and they have consecrated it. The fact of this bay is implanted in their genetic make-up and may exist there as clearly and as profoundly as tender memories are stored in our minds.

It seems then that their message to us, the story they would tell, is about living in the world. About the importance of themselves and of landscapes and how we should imagine them and how we should dream about them. Of how we should invest them with significance and how we should cherish them. It is a story to which we must give metaphoric resonance, symbols, interpretations. We can read into it acts of faith, we can be touched by its poignancy, we can be moved by the sheer accumulation of time that is embodied in each retelling. But we cannot be different. When we stare at their great size in the seas or look up at their skeletons hung from the ceilings of museums, we must respond. We are called upon to feel.

Once, many years ago, I felt compelled to make just this sort of response. On a west-coast beach I was confronted with the remains of a life, with a single rib-bone sticking out of the sand. It was lodged among some rocks exposed by an ebbing tide and must have lain buried against those rocks for years, yet in the wash of the last tide it had been partly uncovered. I felt, sentimentally, that if I claimed it then in my imagination the whale it had been could at least swim on for some more years. So I dug it free and took it down to the shallows to wash off the mussels that clung to it and the fine strands of seagrass that sprouted from its damaged end where a honeycomb of bone tissue was visible.

This whale lives in me. It is part of my dream. I have created for it a bay of still water ringed by granite mountains that are the colour of ash in the harsh light of midday and indigo at twilight. Here this whale can leap as I have watched others leap: breaking from the surface again and again and again, leaving troubled patches of foam in its wake. Here its tail rises from the sea in a symbol of all that is beautiful and strong: an image of celebration.

Here the whale is part of a larger narrative, part of the story that is our conversation with ourselves and the land and the seas. In this we try to describe the awe that is struck in us at the play of lightning in approaching storms, or the arrangement of rocks on a barren plain, or a formation of vultures upon a midday sky. In this we recount our being. It is the story of who we are and what we mean. In it is stored our wisdom. But, more significantly, I think that from its rhythms come our dreams. And perhaps by telling and retelling we may come to know how we should live.

Muizenberg
June–September 1994

Notes

1

Details of the d'Almeida account were taken from Richard Elphick's *Khoikhoi and the Founding of White South Africa* (Johannesburg, Ravan Press, 1985). Eve Palmer's descriptions of Bushman-hunting come from *The Plains of Camdeboo* (London, Fontana, 1974). The words sung by Julie Covington are from Jeff Wayne's *The Musical Version of 'The War of the Worlds'* (CBS Inc., 1978). The quote from *New Statesmen* was taken from issue no. 1 (London, Fleetway Publications, 1989) written by John Smith and illustrated by Jim Baikie. Explanations of various Bushman paintings, including the one described here, are given by David Lewis-Williams and Thomas Dowson in their book *Images of Power, Understanding Bushman Rock Art* (Johannesburg, Southern Book Publishers, 1989). For further details about Jane Alexander's work see *Resistance Art in South Africa* by Sue Williamson (Cape Town, David Philip, 1990). Historical information was taken from *An Illustrated History of South Africa* (Johannesburg, Jonathan Ball Publishers, and Cape Town, Human & Rousseau, 1987) edited by Trewhella Cameron. A yellowtail is a game fish particularly abundant in Cape waters.

2

The interaction between Vladimir and Estragon is in Act 1 of Samuel Beckett's *Waiting for Godot* (London, Faber & Faber,

1970, courtesy of Faber & Faber Ltd and Grove/Atlantic Inc.). The Judge is Judge Johann Kriegler, who headed the Independent Electoral Commission. Some of the details about the IEC's incompetence were taken from the *Cape Times*, 5 May 1994, and the story of Nomaza Paintin from *Rapport*, 12 June 1994. A version of the story on disinvestment appeared in an Argus Leadership publication on sanctions in 1988/89. Additional information was obtained during an interview in July 1994. Black business attitudes in the Western Cape were noted in an interim report by Jill Gallimore based on a Wesgro research project initiated by Wesgro/Montsi Associates, January 1994. Sandile Dikeni's column appeared in the *Cape Times*, 7 May 1994.

3

A version of Howard and Emma's story appeared in a Mondadori publication in Italy in September 1989. I interviewed them again in June 1994.

4

Information about the inauguration of Nelson Mandela as President was taken from the *Cape Times*, 10 May 1994, and the *Weekly Mail & Guardian*, 13 May 1994. Other quotations are from Joseph Conrad's *Heart of Darkness* (New York, Dover Publications, 1990); R. W. Johnson's *How Long Will South Africa Survive?* (Johannesburg, Macmillan Ltd, 1977); 'The Second Coming' by W. B. Yeats from the *Collected Poems of W. B. Yeats* (London, Macmillan, 1971); and from 'Alexandra' by Mongane Wally Serote, which appears in his collection *Yakhal'inkomo* (Johannesburg, Renoster Books, 1974, courtesy of Ad Donker Publishers (Pty) Ltd). The reaction of Robben Island prisoners to the June '76 riots was recorded in *Robben Island*, a BBC-TV Arena production written and directed by Adam Low, April 1994. Details about the first sitting of Parliament were reported in the *Cape Times*, 10 May 1994. The poem 'The Taste of the Fruit' by William Plomer appears in his *Collected Poems* (London, Jonathan Cape, 1973).

5

Quotations from the Bible are from Revelation 6:10 and Isaiah 54:7–8 and 60:18. Also quoted is a short extract from J. M. Coetzee's novel *Age of Iron* (London, Secker & Warburg, 1990). Further information was taken from *The Argus*, 10 June 1994; *Cape Times*, 18 June 1994; R. W. Johnson's article, 'Here for the crunch – R. W. Johnson in South Africa', in the *London Review of Books*, Vol. 16, no. 8, 1994; *Weekly Mail & Guardian*, 15 October 1993, 22 October 1993; *Cape Times*, 16 October 1993; *Vrye Weekblad*, 28 October 1993; *The Argus*, 12 March 1994; *Sunday Times*, 27 March 1994; *Weekend Argus*, 23/24 April 1994; *Weekly Mail & Guardian*, 20 May 1994, 10 June 1994.

6

Details about the trial of the AWB members involved in the roadblock were taken from *The Argus*, 16–21 May 1994; the *Sunday Times*, 22 May 1994; and the *Cape Times*, 18 June 1994. A report on the activities and thoughts of Marguerite Vermeulen appeared in the *Weekly Mail & Guardian*, 17 September 1993. Interviews were conducted during February 1994.

7

Details of the Heidelberg Tavern attack were taken from *The Argus*, 31 December 1993 and 5 January 1994. Interviews with the survivors and the bereaved were conducted in July and August 1994.

8

Quotations are from Frantz Fanon's *The Wretched of the Earth* (London, Penguin, 1982, courtesy of HarperCollinsPublishers

Ltd); the 'Four Quartets' by T. S. Eliot, in *Collected Poems* (London, Faber & Faber, 1970); Noel Mostert's *Frontiers* (New York, Knopf, 1992); J. B. Peires's *The Dead Will Arise* (Johannesburg, Ravan Press, 1989); *Narrative of the Kaffirwar 1850–1851–1852* (Cape Town, C. Struik, 1962) by R. Godlonton and Edward Irving; *The Reminiscences of Thomas Stubbs* (Cape Town, A. A. Balkama, 1978) edited by W. A. Maxwell and R. McGeogh. Further historical information was obtained from the *Graham's Town Journal*, 31 May 1851, 10 June 1851, 14 June 1851; and Cameron's *An Illustrated History of South Africa*. For an account of the Bambatha rebellion see Shula Marks's *Reluctant Rebellion: The 1906–1908 Disturbances in Natal* (Oxford, Clarendon Press, 1970) and *A History of the Zulu Rebellion* (London, MacMillan & Co., 1913) by James Stuart. W. H. Auden's poem 'Spain' appears in *The English Auden* (London, Faber & Faber, 1977).

9

For background to the Israelite uprising see Robert Edgar's booklet *Because They Chose the Plan of God* (Johannesburg, Ravan Press, 1988). The quotations from the Bible are Revelation 6:9–11 and Psalms 83:3–18. A version of the story on the Bondelswart uprising appeared in *Leadership*, Vol. 13, no. 1, 1994. Information for this account was taken from the *Cape Argus*, 19 June 1922; Cameron's *An Illustrated History of South Africa*; *The Star*, 17 May 1921, 10 June 1922; and from personal interviews conducted by James Ambrose Brown in the late Sixties. I am also indebted to his novel, *The Return* (Cape Town, Purnell, 1971). For detailed descriptions of the bombing and final killing of Abram Morris see Richard Freislich's *The Last Tribal War* (Cape Town, C. Struik, 1964).

10

Information was taken from the *Weekly Mail & Guardian*, 13 May 1994; *South*, 10 June 1994; *Weekly Mail & Guardian*, 1

July 1994. The quotations from Vaclev Havel are taken from his keynote address to the Salzburg Music Festival in 1990. Further details are from the *Cape Times*, 11 June 1994, 7 June 1994, 20 June 1994; and *South*, 10 June 1994. Quotations are from Primo Levi's *The Drowned and the Saved* (London, Michael Joseph, 1988); Elisabeth Reichart's novel, *February Shadows* (London, The Women's Press, 1988); and *The White Devil* (London, Ernest Benn Ltd, 1971) by John Webster.

Envoi

Slavenka Drakulić's observations come from her book *How we Survived Communism and Even Laughed* (London, Vintage, 1993). Further information was taken from *The Star*, 25 July 1994; and the *Cape Times*, 30 July 1994, 2 August 1994, 3 August 1994. The quotations from the *New York Times* appeared in *The Argus*, 4 August 1994. Excerpts from Leonard Cohen's lyrics were taken from his CD *The Future* (Columbia, 1993) and from the songs 'Anthem' (copyright © 1992 Leonard Cohen Stranger Music Inc.) and 'Democracy' (copyright © 1992 Leonard Cohen Stranger Music Inc.). The reviewer mentioned is Leon Wieseltier writing in the *New Yorker* of 26 July 1993 under the headline: 'The Prince of Bummers'. Quotations are from W. H. Auden's poem 'Spain' in *The English Auden*.